Omnipresence of Money

Dr. Ebenezer Robinson, PhD

ISBN:13:978-1497427969
ISBN:10:1497427967

DEDICATION

This book is dedicated to the Lord Jesus Christ. Jesus Christ is my GOD and my SAVIOR. I worship, praise, and thank you Lord Jesus Christ for the gift of eternal life. Thank you for standing by me every step of the way.

Money is just a tool (or legal tender)

CONTENTS

ACKNOWLEDGMENTS

I would like to take this opportunity to express my heartfelt gratitude to all who helped me complete this book. Their comments and suggestions were a large part of the success of this book. I am also extremely appreciate of my entire family. I would like to thank my late mom and dad, Dorcas and Emmanuel who always had faith in everything I did. I wish they were here to share in this achievement. Finally, I would like to thank all my friends, Facebook friends and family, and people at work, coffee shops, stores, and the public at large, for their support, patience, and listening to my endless rapports about this book over a period of years, without wish I could never have completed this book. Thank you all for believing in me

CHAPTER 1
Twitter and Email Marketing Campaign

Internet has spawned the twenty-four hours shopping liberty for the enjoyment of consumers and small business owners. Shoppers are now enjoying no time limit of services offered by the convenience of e-commerce business transactions. Several organizations are now actively participating on e-commerce business. On a global scale, online vendors do seize e-commerce profitable and cost efficient opportunities. As consumers we are continually offered products and services via the Internet. In our jobs, no matter what profession we are in, E-Commerce is being used more and more to conduct business, for training purposes and daily communications. This book provides introduction to E-Commerce as small business owners utilize revenue models, it focuses on omnipresence of money of E-Commerce, technology infrastructure, and it describes business concepts and customer relationships. This book is designed specifically for small business owner launching a business and it discusses E-Commerce in action by focusing on real-world E-Commerce experience in small business owners, retail, twitter & email marketing, incentive programs, customers' retention, communication, web site traffic, and viral marketing. The general public is cognizance of the inalienable right and privileges arrogated to the entire citizen from the Constitution of United States. In the world of the Internet, the public is now acclimatized to how effective an email marketing campaigns has provided immense freedom to the sole proprietors and consumer. This technology has made it possible for global customers to use their finances to procure a variety of services and commodities. One is now familiar with how the Internet has spawned the twenty-four hours liberty to the online company and consumers to sell and purchase products and services thus contributing to better standards of living. The global society enjoys almost unlimited products and services offered through the convenience of email marketing, and Internet transactions and time is no longer a factor. Several single mothers and sole proprietors are now actively participating in twitter (email) marketing campaigns; and they are accumulating millions of dollars from the omnipresence of money via e-commerce. On a global scale, online small business owners should seize the profitable and cost efficient e-commerce opportunities.

Meanwhile, according to the Merriam-Webster Dictionary effort, brain or mind of human being is responsible for the manifestations of opinion, idea, suggestion, invention, process or intellectual property (Merriam-Webster Dictionary 11th Collegiate Dictionary). Internet has developed new areas of intellectual property rights, privacy and information rights for consumers and merchants. Shoppers are now enjoying twenty-four hours and seven days a week retailing offered by the convenience of e-commerce business transactions. The body of this book will articulate about the necessities and repercussions of online intellectual property rights, privacy, information rights, financial services, travel services, auctions, portals, community, supply chain management, collaborative commerce, and digital media.

We have seen how Internet and e-commerce has given vast freedom to the consumer and merchant. This technology has made it possible for global customers to use their finances to procure variety of commodities. One is now familiar with how Internet has spawned the twenty-four hours liberty to the consumers to procure amenities thus contributing to good standard of living. Global society enjoys no limit of the products and services offered by the convenience of e-commerce business transactions and time is no longer the issue. Several organizations are now actively participating in e-commerce business and enjoying the capitalism. On a global scale, online vendors do seize e-commerce profitable and cost efficient opportunities.

The book will let you peruse how Internet has produced new areas of dilemma with intellectual property rights,

Privacy and information rights for consumers and merchants. How the convenience of e-commerce business transactions has globally changed the life of the society. This book has articulated about the provisions and current status of intellectual property rights and the Internet, privacy and information rights, on-line financial services, travel services, auctions and portals community, supply chain management, collaborative commerce, and digital media.

This book has articulated how Internet banking is a success in every measure. The purposes of this research has been served in the realms of how banking industries supports the concepts of Internet banking logistics, benefits, remunerations; price and endowment; article of trade; distribution; pricing strategies; and promotional campaign, online security compliance, Conditions, findings and recommendations. Meanwhile, Internet has developed new lucrative areas of online banking. Accordingly, the security innovations are noted in the body of this book because organization management has recently implemented procedures to ensure that all the security promulgations are complied with.

In the evolving world of the electronic commerce the public knows that email, tweet, and text are the primary medium of competitive advantage to retail products and services to online customers. In an email (or twitter)-oriented marketing campaign, the entrepreneur initiating a new business procures an email (tweeter) list in a lawfully and morally responsible method. The global model for entrance into the world of online business calls for designing a marketing strategy and implementing that strategy with the thought process of online customer behavior. In the following few pages, this book will discuss the primary attributes of an effective email (or twitter) -oriented marketing campaign. Having said that, let us look into how to build relationships of trust with prospective customers.

In the environment of email and (or twitter) marketing campaign several organizations create stronger bonds with prospective customer through a concept known as customer relationship management (CRM). Specifically, this is a situation of handling a detailed dossier about individual users and carefully extending gratuity with the end purpose of maximizing consumer conversion. Similarly, the electronic customer relationship management (eCRM) enhances organization value and elicits customer enjoyment. Likewise, this concept holds that eCRM is cost effective, maximizes sales, enables superior market targeting and generates customer rapport; educe relationship and personalization. The online business owner should adjust eCRM systems to rehabilitate customer service, retain clients and assist in accruing well thought out capabilities on the Web site.

To some extent, online business owner must resolve each desire of specific consumers, solve customer problems and embark on erecting consumer loyalty, trust and lifetime value. Meanwhile, after creating a well-defined market, online business owner should focus on customer desires, organize whatever that will positively encourage customers, and grow revenue by gratifying consumers. In order to build relationship with customers, online business owner should familiarize consumers with customization, personalize marketing, customer co-production, compelling content and customer service such as CRMs, FAQs, virtual chat, intelligent agents and programmed response systems. At this point, let us look into the attributes of an effective email (or twitter)-oriented marketing campaign and how to manage email lists.

According to several scholars, the attributes of an effective email and twitter oriented marketing campaign should enable small business owners to influence prospective consumers for the purchase of products or services. In order to have influence on the prospective consumer the business owner must have contact with them through variety of media. Meanwhile, they should eradicate the panic of interacting with the prospective clients who are ignorant of the offerings. Likewise, small business owners should employ interpersonal skills to make a significant impact on prospective customers. However, to be effective in the marketing campaign the online owner should operate the following activities: (a) exemplify mission in action, (b) epitomize passion (c) elicit compassion, (d) give out free products, coupon, rebate (e) rapport about products or services, (f) typify stability, commitment and consistent and (g) assist customers. Conversely, online business owner should often utilize email messages to inculcate branding, convert new consumers and maintain life-long loyalty of customers.

The concept of managing email lists acknowledged that adherence to List Server is mandatory for the online small business owners because the implementation will help them to amass email and twitter addresses. In addition, this List Server maintains each separate mailing list while spontaneously processing customer approval and disapproval requisitions. Online business owners are encouraged to coach consumer and also take the advantage of Webcast, Blogs and other multimedia to discuss the benefits, necessity and use of their products and services. Having said that, let us look into the marketing goals in email-oriented marketing.

The marketing goal depicts what a particular business owner wants to accomplish, however, the marketing strategy describes how to accomplish that goal. Every business must create a strategy for accomplishing its goal. The marketing goal of most organizations includes sales maximization, market-share increase, profit attainability, risk eradication, enhancement and reputation preservation. Meanwhile, the online business owner might decide that the goal for two years is to reduce expenses, increase revenue and maximize profit. Similarly, another objective is to increase business owner market share and prices in order to maximize revenue.

Consequently, online business owner should quantify the goals and objectives in order to derive profitability benefit. For example, organization may want to devise goals by intending to maximize the return on investment by 20 percent within a year. Conversely, administration should find the interest, desires, needs, and wants of customers. They also need to deliver the expected gratifications more effectively and professionally than other competitive business owner. All successful organization delivers gratifications in a special way that safeguards or maximizes consumer standard of living. However, online business owner should have customer service employees that are knowledgeable of the business concept and ready to provide information and ease the novices of online users. On the whole, the public conceded that organization should embark on a responsible email targeting, Opt-in permission marketing and the business use of email systems. In addition, successful companies are compliant with policies predicated on obtaining prior consent and clear agreement of the email recipients. At this point, let us peruse the tip sheets in email marketing campaign.

The concept of the Online-marketing campaign calls for business owners to compel the email recipient to assent by purchasing product. The web site owner would send link oriented confirmation e-mail to the prospective customer that consented to the opt-ins, and ask the individual to click the link to confirm. Similarly, the personal email is the best tool for online business owner to embark on when conveying promotions or newsletters to prospects or customers.

The list management tool such as List-Mate helps online business owners to implement removal request, handle vast email lists, and amass users address lists. However, the powerful email promotions are convenient system to dispense compelling messages to vast recipients on a global scale. After all, small business owner can utilize email to encourage discussion groups to compel consumer traffic to the Web site, there is probability that users will revisit the Web site to update responses and perhaps purchase products from the company. For example, the promotional email messages will enable the consumers to try the following: (a) adopt newsletters, (b) order and purchase merchandise, (c) adopt promotional presentations, (d) allow users to revisit, and (e) adopt Web concepts. Many scholars encourage business owner to embed free software tip sheets on the email messages or on the Web site because this will persuade consumers to revisit the site, peruse professional software tip sheets, assimilate promotional messages, and perhaps purchase product. Having said that, let us peruse the strategies of email-oriented marketing campaign and the role of the Web in business information system.

Single mothers looking to increase their profits or sales should expend less money, time and resources to grow new customers. To convert consumers, the online companies are encouraged to position advertisements on the email, online, and multimedia stimulate the prospective recipients. The optimum goal of the effective marketing campaign is to sends direct mail, email, pop ups, banners, paste advertisements on billboards and makes phone calls to probable new prospects. The sales people are known to engage in free trade shows to find new consumers. The subsequent agenda is to find which prospective customers are authentic prospects, to decipher this they conduct questionnaires and financial standing surveys, and so on. The online business owner that has a need for quick customer response to the advertisements must schedule a moderate time limit for the due date for the cancellation of the product on sale.

Surprisingly, email continues to be the most operative type of online promotion in terms of click-through rate. A functional Web site that prospective customers can discover is one of the strongest online communications tools. The following are all vital parts of a coordinated marketing communications strategy: Appropriate domain name-companies should select a domain name that is short, memorable, hard to confuse or misspell, and indicative of a firm's business functions, and that preferably uses dot.com as its top-level domain. In conjunction with marketing campaign each business owner should ensure that the sales representatives increase new customers and new market on a daily basis.

Whereas, to obtain customer profiles and behavior online business owner employs cookies, transaction logs, shopping cart, data mining, database, data warehouses and CRM systems. However, profiling technologies provide significant revenue benefit but online business owner must apply discretion with this vast information. Online companies should utilize compelling advertisement strategies, such as, one grand prize winner wins: (a) $500, (b) 4 weeks beach house vacation, (c) two thousand dollars, (d) win instant cash prizes from $10 - $200 (e) if you buy two products you may win $100 cash, and (f) to register customers should insert one code entry per day on the Web site. Having said that, let us peruse building consumer relationships and using a brochure Web site to tell a story as it evolves.

The best way to satisfy prospective customers is when their email questions or requests receive immediate attention without too much delay. The online business owner may even apply the system of automatic e-mail response to get customers feel appreciated. To build consumer relationship corporation should rearrange customer waiting time and commit to timely delivery of products consequently consumers will revisit the Web site to make additional purchases. For example, in building consumer relationship, Amazon and Yahoo organization elicit lessons on how to enable consumer loyalty and relationships. Similarly, satisfied customers will be loyal to a particular company, and in turn become return customers to buy additional products.

Loyal customers usually defend the product of the company, may also upgrades on current products and new merchandise. When consumers are not satisfied they will decline to make a purchase or even become second-time buyers. When organization makes the commercial process easy by resolving issues, by responding quickly to consumers, by listening and solving customer complaints as a result retain more customers.

The brochure Web site is the primarily constructed to introduce a business offerings, contact, and to give an excellent outlook on the administrators, products and the industry. The brochure Web site permit corporation to update, display, integrates video clips, audio clips and other multimedia. Nevertheless, let corporation arise and confer value and respect upon consumers. Finally, to maintain a professional attitude, demeanor and build consumer relationship online corporation should recognize his or her customers by giving them certificate of appreciation. Having said that, let us now look into how to make incentive programs easy and Web-based electronic commerce.

The advent of e-commerce changed the online business orientation with five different types of e-commerce. Consequently, one is now familiar with (B2C) business-to-consumer e-commerce - describe company online that sells to shoppers, the standing example is Amazon.com. The next type is known as (B2B) business-to-business e-commerce – refer to company online that transacts business with each other, specifically with supplier; a popular example that comes to mind is ChemConnect.com. The third type is known as (C2C) consumer-to-consumer e-commerce – is the category where shopper conduct business with each other, an example that come to mind is ebay. The fourth type is called (P2P) peer-to-peer e-commerce - is the sort where people exchange music files with each while bypassing central web server. Finally, the mobile commerce - is the type where users can use wireless digital devices like blackberries to conduct business on the Internet.

One thing abundantly clear is that the world witnessed the advent of (B2C) around March 1992; meanwhile, the notion of (B2C) was fully entrusted to the society through Netscape browser in year of 1994 and with the participation of Amazon.com in the year 1995. In addition, (B2C) started with the traditional sales of commodities however today (B2C) has evolved to offer varieties of commodities and services, for instance (B2C) now carries travel agencies like Travelocity.com, Expedia.com, and Priceline.com.

Moreover, (B2C) now offer online banking, automobile sales, life insurance sales, car insurance, real estate marketing, educational services, and other goods and services needed by the society. Conversely, the technical progression of Internet has minimized the expenses of (B2B), thus, small businesses are currently enjoying the privileges offer by the Internet. Financially (B2B) still supersedes and maintain the principal e-commerce functions. Governments have recognized the advantages of e-commerce. As a result, (G2C) government to consumer, (C2G) consumer to government, (G2B) government to business and (B2G) business to government sites have sprung up at the Federal, state, and local levels.

One should be aware that (C2C) limelight began in 1995 the period eBay.com was inaugurated. (C2C) is the type of e-commerce where a consumer can actually act as both the seller and buyer; however, their business transaction materializes via an intermediary. Society is now conversant with the example of (C2C) such as online auction web site like (eBay.com, uBid.com, Overstock.com to name a few). The doctrine and the profitability of e-commerce have persuaded the Governments. Consequently, (G2C), (C2G), (G2B) and (B2G) sites have obviously manifested at the Federal, state, and local levels. For example, the U.S. government can boast of one of the prominent government e-business web sites that are normally controlled by the IRS to provide information, (G2C), and tax return filing (C2G).

An astute observer is bound to recognize that the epoch of e-commerce (I) began in 1995 through 2001. Technological innovation contributed to the phenomenal growth of the e-commerce (I). This was a period when website was used to advertise company products and all the dot.com company's stock value that eventually collapse. Whereas the e-commerce (II) inauguration began in January 2001, hence the management of e-commerce (II) companies innovatively brought the successful campaign of order and rationality to the online industry this period transformed the online business because it depicted the reconstruction of online enterprise and aggrandizes the stock prices and value.

We discovered that e-commerce (I) activated the following manifestations (A) Technology-driven (B) Revenue growth emphasis (C) Venture capital financing (D) Ungoverned (E) Entrepreneurial (F) Disintermediation (G) Perfect markets (H) Pure online strategies (I) First mover advantages, whereas the e-commerce (II) proffer the (A) Business driven (B) Earnings and profit emphasis (C) Traditional financing (D) Stronger regulation and governance (E) Large traditional firms (F) Strengthening intermediaries (J) Imperfect markets, brands, network effects (H) Integrated. (I) Multi-channel (K) Bricks-and-click strategies (L) Strategic follower strength (M) Complimentary assets.

In my organization sometimes they do have frequent computer upgrades for example we recently went through what we call Network Implementation Project (NIP), this projects provides a complete re-design and upgrade of the Organization's Network Infrastructure. The organization Information Technology Department (ITD) crafted a schedule for the upgrade for the duration of five consecutives working days. Throughout this period ITD reconfigured the existing computers and printers onto a new wiring plant and network infrastructure. On scheduled days, data connectivity on specified departments are lost as data systems are moved over to the new network.

This means that employees will not have access to email, the Internet, data files or networked applications. Employees were required to backup data and make necessary preparations to use manual processes until the network becomes available on the scheduled day. One thing is abundantly clear this network upgrade greatly enhances the performance and reliability of email, the Internet, data files or networked applications by adding increased capacity and eliminated redundancy. In modern companies this is one of several necessary steps in continuing effort to improve services and ability to serve better.

The following representations are the key elements of the business model: specifically, proposition, revenue model, market opportunity, competitive environment, competitive advantage, market strategy, organizational development, and management team. One would find that the representations of business model are noteworthy because they are paramount for stimulating booming business in any realm including e-commerce. The definition of value proposition is the enjoyment derivable when a company's product extended satisfaction to vast customers. The e-commerce changed business orientation because shoppers have the advantage to personalize, normalize and customize their individual product, and they also have the convenience to purchase product on a twenty-four hours basis.

In addition, e-commerce now allows merchandiser to enjoy low cost of advertisement, operation, and delivery and amass profitable revenue. The e-commerce model of revenue, advertising, subscription, marketing, transaction, fee, sales, and affiliate did transform business on a global scale. Netflix online company provides an outstanding example how e-commerce has transformed businesses and new company can now survive the rigor of the competitive atmosphere. Online product costs effectiveness, customer care, timeliness of product delivery, specification and customization of product are essential factors in online value proposition to consumers.

Furthermore, the innovations of e-commerce value propositions that transform business are derived from the society trend, whim and the state of the economy. For example, Amazon.com makes it possible for book lovers to shop for virtually any book in hard copy or e-book from the comfort of their home or office, 24 hours a day, and to know immediately whether a book is in stock. Amazon primary value propositions are unparalleled selection and convenience. Organization should always strive to satisfy the desires of the consumer. E-commerce brought about the innovation of advertising revenue whereby a company that owns space on the websites obtains fees from vast online and traditional advertisers. This business novelty made it possible so that the higher the users of the websites the higher the amount the owner of the website can charge the advertisers.

Consequently, e-commerce created the originality of online subscription revenue, thus Yahoo website offers its client vast amount of first-rate services and charges subscription fee of $5.95 a month for Yahoo! Plus, where the users enjoy the benefit of high-class online movies, brand new music videos, games, radio and massive storage email account. E-commerce implemented transaction revenue so the world of business online company like ebay.com get vast fee from seller whenever the individual sells an item. In addition, when customer procures a stock etrade.com collect transaction fee as online stockbroker. Sales revenue protocol is now in the field of online business, for instance, Amazon.com and half.com get revenue by selling online books, music, movies, videos and other product.

E-commerce produced the modernization of affiliate revenue hence such companies like MyPoint.com divert customers to the partners companies and get recompense of great reward of revenue, fees and percentage of sales. In addition, epinion.com redirects businesses to associate companies and receive revenue. E-commerce brought about the market opportunity then new online company may now choose their own section of market-space. For instance, new company have the chances to sell its products to vast numbers of small business firms who can only afford to spend $6 billion on computer software training even though they still yearn for low cost training resolution.

One is now familiar with the competitive environment that spells out the thought process of finding out the existing competitors before new company enter the online markets-pace. Society is now cognizance that the competitive advantage speaks about the privileges any firm is bringing to the online market-space. Market strategy is all about the plan in store to advertise organization products or services to the target audience. Organizational development speaks about the kind of organization hierarchy available in the firm and the importance of their responsibilities to implement business plan. Management team should elucidate about the style of proficiency, expertise and education essential for the organizational leadership.

The web has enabled new business opportunities such as online multi-channels business enterprise, for example in my organization coworkers normally purchases their commodities from many channels via the telephone, email, internet, television and in store. We are all aware of coworkers who got the houses financed from low interest e-loan. Car insurance is compulsory in the State of Texas, one thing is certain, the cheapest premium are gotten from the e-insurance. The business models available in the e-commerce have revolutionized business on many forums. Thus, Internet being an equal opportunity technology has given easy access to competitor thereby making room for stronger competition. That being said, consumers now possess more buying powers because of the abundant information on the e-commerce therefore buyers can now disburse for inexpensive product from online merchandiser. Meanwhile, Internet is now creating quality, excellence, value, in order to brand online products and exacting premium prices. On the Web one should be expected to find brick and wall business like Wal-Mart or Sears.

One thing is noteworthy, when a company craft efficient e-commerce business model the result would be, competitive advantage, productivity and higher income. Thus, one should be cognizance of the prominent e-commerce business models examples like Yahoo, eBay, IBM, Apple, and many others. Business model is popularly known and defined as an instrument through which organization produces revenue, profit and meet the needs of the variety of customers. Whereas, some other sector define business models as the preplanned way of doing business and deliberately implemented to manifest profit in a marketplace. Meanwhile, in order to craft or improve on an e-commerce business model, business entities that indicate special resources would magnify the commodities value and insulate the company from competitors. Special resource might be e-commerce technology, brand name, durability of product, quality of commodities and services.

The corporation must emphasize to the prospective customers to act now when the email lies unattended to in the inbox because prospective consumers may eventually delete it thereby refuses to respond to the marketing messages. Thus, business owner should advocate the tendency of urgency to drive immediate response from the prospective clients. Online corporation should take the advantage and appropriate the benefits that come through the concept of act now. Embedding a time frame of reference on the offering, such as, for a limited time only will also stimulate the sense of urgency of the call-to-response. Through the email messages, business owner should compel the recipient to comply with the sales solicitation.

The majority of businesses that are successful achieve it because their mode of operation follows the concept of honoring the prospective customers on a consistent basis. In contrast, many consumers are aware the obligations of online corporation drive to provide urgent promotional messages and end it with an email hotlinks. For example, famous companies like Amazon.com rely on hotlink to collect consumer tastes, buying preferences, book titles, offer free gifts, discount, rebate and enlisted topics. These services and recompense perform effectively. In choosing an e-commerce service, the concept acknowledges that situations arise where a business owner must maximize profitability; the expectation is that the business owner would procure e-commerce that permit quick incoming payment, secure order, prompt order response and adequate security.

Search engine optimization-companies should register with all the major search engines so that a user looking for comparable sites has a better chance of finding that particular site; ensure that keywords used in the Web site description match keywords likely to be utilized as search terms by prospective customers; and connect the site to as many other sites as possible. Web site functionality-once at a Web site, prospective customers need to be enticed to stay and to purchase. Web site design features that impact online purchasing include how compelling the experience of using the Web site is, download time, product list navigation, the number of clicks needed to purchase, the presence of customer choice agents, and the Web site's responsiveness to customer needs.

Studies have shown that low click-through rates are not suggestive of a lack of commercial impact of online advertising, and that advertising communication does occur even when prospective customers do not directly respond by clicking. Online advertising in its innumerable forms has been shown to increase brand awareness and brand recall, create brand perceptions, and increase intent to purchase. The implicit and explicit suggestion includes setting the deadline directly or indirectly in the tone of the advertisement messages so that the prospective customers can respond on a timely basis. Researchers have discovered that unmotivated prospective customers will allow their messages to park in the in box and eventually delete it.

A big challenge outstanding is how to collect personal information. Currently, there are three popular approaches- direct consumer solicitations, explicit feedback and collecting personal information during online registration. While explicit approach identifies personal interests by mining consumers Web browsing behavior recorded in Web logs. Other compelling form of effectiveness on the Web site includes companies permitting consumers to design or personalize merchandise; this allows business owner to dispense differentiated goods to each consumer, this is positive empowerment that permits consumers to design preferences. For examples, the Procter & Gamble's reflection.com has a Web site that permits shoppers to design beauty products. Conversely, another authority emphasized how prospective customers are discouraged and not impressed because of the audacity of deadline connotation.

Make certain that all email recipients are treated as one segment, thus, give them identical offers one thing is certain, an implicit and explicit suggestion bring about the most effective online marketing campaign. Meanwhile, in constructing elements a business owner should incorporate these elements on the Web site (a) contact forms, (b) guest books, (c) discussions boards, (d) voting board, (e) information request, opinion forms, complain form and appointment calendar. Visitors revisit the Web site because the elements are attractive and inviting.

On the whole, majority of the scholars endorses the following guideline concerning email campaign on the Web site resources: Respect the privacy of users. Do not seek information about, obtain copies of, or modify electronic information belonging to other users unless explicitly authorized to do so by those users. The distribution of promotional contents, programs, databases, email content and other electronic information resources is usually controlled by the laws of copyrights, licensing agreements and trade secret laws. Corporation is hereby advice to observe the letter and the spirit of these laws to safeguard against liability litigations. Let us now look into how to create convincing and compelling messages and managing graphics for maximum impact.

To make an absolute impact on the consumers, convincing and compelling messages should be in the active voice, rather than in the passive voice, although this is not absolute in some cases the passive voice may be more appropriate in certain circumstances. The following are the way to make a message more compelling: (a) highlight the primary value (b) authenticate the benefits of products and (c) magnify the advantages of the services to the prospective consumers. Meanwhile, keep in mind that the personal computer is a known vehicle for communication that belongs to the prospective clients. Thus, the contents and the tone of the sale messages emanating from the business owner should be congruent with decency and courtesy. The implication is that if a business owner disregards advancing compelling messages to consumers, this business will soon be listed in the book of bankruptcy.

In managing graphics for maximum impact, the concept holds that the goal is to completely eradicate Web site slow downloads and maximize ease of navigation, appropriate color, precise sound configuration and legible font sizes. Business owner should ensure that graphic image contents have precision measurement. Business owner is best advice to reutilize the graphic image contents in order to be conservative on Internet download. The business owner will enjoy advantages such as obtaining customer dossier, email address, financial statistics, understanding buying behavior and other vital statistics.

To foster a positive Web frequent visit, according to several scholars, each online business owner will be responsible for growing customers. For example, online corporation should adhere to consumer preferences such as maintaining inexpensive shipping, privacy, timely delivery, off-line return, recompense, off-line location, refund, protecting dossier, and safeguarding credit cards. Having said that, let us now look into how conciseness is the essence of business and using enhancement to promote stickiness.

When probing for information on products and services, business owner usually finds that Internet customers loath to peruse a huge amount of information. The online consumers prefer the information to be concise and straight to the point. Prospective consumers are preoccupy and the business owner should take this into consideration. The email messages should be concise as possible and get to the point or else the online prospects will move to other competitors.

Marketing promotions should be as concise as possible while still conveying the messages intended to the prospective customers. Concurrently, characteristics of effective messages should include at least the following: (a) indispensable benefit of the products, (b) benefit of services proffers (c) valuable and (d) active. One is now convinced that concise content are coherent, helps users gain awareness, carry authentic tone, responding to diverse situations, clarity and cohesive. In contrast, the content factors on the Web site encourage customer repeat visits. Hence, keep the content interesting, concise, useful and continuously adapting.

Utilize content to attract first-time users and to bring the visitor back again, for example, many organizations prefer the following: (a) substantial information including links to related Web sites, (b) permit varying news of interest, (c) varying free offers to users, (d) updates contests and sweepstakes, (e) permit humor and jokes, and (f) offer free games. In the realms of ecommerce, one thing is abundantly clear conciseness is the sole of business. In discussion of using enhancement to promote stickiness, the concept calls upon business owner to combine effort to promote consumer revisit to the Web site through the success of stickiness.

Accordingly, company and workforce are encourage to be proactive participant to promote the overall stickiness by providing the availability of interesting games, community newsletter, chat rooms, virtual interactive, stock quotes, meteorological services, sound and video clips on the Web site. Accordingly, Web sites may provide a strategy for users to continually response to a poll or discussion in order to keep users revisits for information or products.

CHAPTER 2
Incentive Programs

The online business owners are absolutely convinced that if companies want to obtain a spontaneous response from the email promotion of the prospective customers, the inclusion of the key words such as, free trial, sample, product, discount and limited time offers will activate rapid responses. Incentives should prompt customers to revisit the Web site. For instance, the authentic incentives that will satisfy customers include online club membership, product customization and personalized gifts. Concurrently, sales promotion is a paramount ingredient to elicit urgent procurement of products or services. Meanwhile, the tenet of advertising gives consumers reasons to buy products while sales promotions confer an incentive to procure products.

The online companies are currently seizing the majority of these incentive tools for product promotion, for instance, these incentive tools are offer to consumers: (a) samples, (b) coupons, (c) cash refund, (d) offers, and (e) prices off. In addition, other incentive tools offer are: (a) premium, (b) prices, (c) patronage rewards, (d) free trials, (e) warranties, (f) tie-in promotion price off, (g) cross promotion, (h) point-of-purchase display, (i) demonstration; trade promotion and business and sale-force promotions. Upper management is now an ardent proponent of promotions as an effective sales tool and customers' incentive program. Consequently, to make the incentive program an effective marketing campaign, the online business owner should consider incorporating individualized incentive allocation. Simultaneously, companies should establish a policy regarding customer incentive programs and recognition awards. The policy should recognize and acknowledge exemplary customers.

Companies should allocate incentives such as free products to the prospective customers in the identified areas. In addition, incentives or awards are appropriate when company allocate it for at least four times a year with the award period defined by the executive manager of the company. However, Customers have supremacy; they are always right and are the final arbiter of business decisions. In effective email marketing campaign, online corporation shall acquire, and retain consumers to promote and ensure success in reducing attrition rate of customers.

The concept of Web-based electronic commerce mentioned that the Internet technology began in 1996 from that time people demanded to know about consumer behavior concerning the use of the Web for commerce. The higher the sales of merchandise when a company utilizes old fashion catalog, the higher the indication of sales and revenue when the company adopts the Web-based electronic commerce. When consumers prefer shopping on a global scale an entrepreneur needs to seize the advantage via electronic commerce.

E-commerce model has changed the business because the function represents the potential revenue and non-revenue. Thus, the cogent monetary results included revenue that are increased because of the capacity growth and price differentiation, cost that are minimized because of the clever-way of reducing cost of good and operating cost, and minimization of asset carrying cost because of the management of the cost of working capital and/or fixed asset. However, the non-revenue that creates value may include a variety of visible or invisible results that may materialized because of the e-commerce implementation, for instance, products and services continuous quality improvement, short and quick product delivery schedule, state of the art customer satisfaction, worldwide extension of products services and information, availability and permanency of information. Ingredient such as value proposition model, value-added e-commerce offering supporting resources, revenue model, cost models and value creation could be utilized to craft a new e-commerce model and improve on current e-commerce models. Narrated ingredients are indispensable for developing well-organized e-commerce business models that will satisfy purchaser's aspiration, to cause higher business performance and to maintain organizational competitive edge via e-commerce.

Society knows that jobs are changing. They are impacted by ongoing workplace changes, new technologies, and are rapidly becoming more knowledge based. To keep up will require continuous learning on employee part - an investment both on and off the job. Since training and development is a shared responsibility for both worker and the employer, organization commitment is to provide employee with lifelong learning opportunities. For example my organization offer intranet courses in Technology, Business Management, Safety and Technical training. Organization that implements this aspect of training can help workforce increase value, versatility, and career potential. Job performance and job satisfaction will improve. And, employee will be better able to achieve personal and career goals.

Improving the performance of organization is a major part of employees' job. One should know that it is a difficult task to focus on in the midst of change, resource constraints, and uncertainty. Employee training can do a lot to identify the key business goals and challenges, and then prescribe specific learning activities to help achieve those goals. However, research on leading edge organizations and today's workforce reveals two things one should know. First, investing in the development of a professional, versatile workforce is the best defense against changing and uncertain times. And second, employees today know the work environment is changing and expect to be trained and kept current by their employer. Having said that, Let us look into the important factors that a manager needs to consider when construction an e-commerce site.

One thing remarkable is that website does contain basic web server software in order to respond to consumer requisition from HTML & XML pages. Arguably, constructing a website from the initial stage to the end is more appropriate in terms of ease and inexpensive, however, one should not rehabilitate the wheels of the old website. The organizational management should be cognizance that the best software to be considered for the development of website is popularly known as Apache. In addition, volume of consumers that populate e-commerce site could eventually crash the website. Thus, manager needs to procure IBM WebSphere Commerce Professional Edition. Furthermore, manager should consider allowing the following IBM suite of tools to operate on IBM Pseries Unix-based computer servers: (1) WebSphere Application Server, (2) WebSphere Commerce, and (3) MQ Series Integrater. Cost benefit assumption would have one believe that when building a website it is inexpensive to keep one vendor such as IBM. Interestingly, the hardware that would be needed should amount to ten Web server Pentium 4.2 GHz computer processors and with ten processors the Website could handle more than 100, 000 concurrent users.

The World Wide Web is a group of Internet site all connected by search engines providing access to different information. Whereas, the Internet is a very large computer network made up of thousands of smaller network interacting to governmental, academic, business or entertainment. The World Wide Web is an Internet technology that permits people to access more than 6 billion plus web pages. Internet is a technology that integrates millions of individual computer into available network that enhances global communication between different demography and organizations. Let us now peruse the e-commerce security atmosphere and ways to curb the e-commerce security threats.

Amazingly, when people conduct business on the Internet they are confronted with the lack of security on credit card payment systems. Whenever there is business engagement between the purchaser and merchant on the Internet it is hard to know whether it is legitimate or not. One should now be aware that users are being exposed to lack of privacy and security. There is no way to decipher whether the merchant you are dealing with is authentic or criminal element located in the penitentiary. Shoppers could become a victim of credit card identity fraud or be using stolen credit cards. The merchant is liable when customers cancel credit cards charges after the commodities have been delivered or the product downloaded from the Internet.

The gravity of cybercrime is not fathomable at this moment however criminal activity perpetrated against e-commerce, online consumers and merchants are enormous. Thus, the people that occupy high echelon of e-commerce organization must find decisive resolutions. Society is now cognizant of the scope of security dilemma when doing business on the Internet, such as integrity of information illustrates that a perpetrator might sabotage consumer financial instrument and divulge classified dossier on the web site. Repudiation might occur hence consumer may deny charges or cancel payment on the products previously ordered. Authenticity security problem ensue mostly because of the difficulty to validate the true identity of the shoppers or merchants.

As far as confidentiality problems are concern, the Internet user classified information may be parading multiple web sites. Unauthorized individual or entities can peruse email correspondence. Privacy issues is another security problem such as propriety information communicated in course of online business engagement may be exchanged with unauthorized organization or criminal elements. Availability is also a security problem that entails web site closure and inaccessible. Phishing problem include a situation where criminal perpetrator deceptively collect confidential information on the Internet for financial enrichment. Hacking and cyber-vandalism is a notorious dilemma of deliberately sabotaging a web site.

Credit card fraud/theft is one of the nefarious activities that may prevent several consumers from e-commerce transactions. The problem of spoofing may ensue when criminal hackers disguise their identities; they normally transfer false e-mail addresses otherwise reroute a web link to a wrong address from the one requested and wrong address or site camouflaged as the intended destination.

When it comes to the issues of service attack this problem entails a criminal hacker using the strategy of deluging and saturating a web site with redundant traffic in order to sabotage the network, impairing the web site, closing down the web site, and eventually spoiling consumer affinity. Sniffing is another dilemma that is tantamount to intercepting personal data from the network or publicizing the collected information on multiple web sites.

Inside job is a jeopardy that may confront e-commerce for instance employees who are privy to sensitive organizational information may eventually use them for nefarious activities or perhaps for financial enrichment. Poorly designed server and client software is another problem essentially when the software is too sophisticated it will eventually result in imperfection for a hacker to assail. Lastly, malicious code such as viruses, worms, Trojan horse and bot networks are serious problem to computer operation and reliability. Malicious code usually corrupts how the computer system operates and defaces the information created on the system. The universal caveat that seems to be commonly popular with several users is unawareness of data origination, sources and location. Thus, the problem of data impersonation needs to be absolutely resolved.

In addition, confidence is also needed for the question of whether Internet phone calls will continue to function, email services will continue to operate and electronic commerce business will not be sabotaged by variety of hackers. One thing is certain for the remedy of technology mishap, consumers should develop plan for disruption caused by security problem if they would continue to conduct business on Internet. Society use fire escape and smoke detector the same wisdom will work well to forestall security problem and technological disaster. Thus, the following are best practices for consumers: device a backup copies for family pictures instead of uploading it only on the Internet, secure book copies of monthly bank statement in the house this is good when online banking is not feasible.

Society is noted for being highly dependent on Web site network without being cognizance for Internet security failure. Meanwhile, several Internet hackers have exerted effort to sabotage it but thanks goodness Internet is still functioning. Web sites haven been disrupted. E-mail has been visited with several Spam. Web sites has been congested and slowed down with computer worms. Fortunately, the Internet has been victorious over several attacks perpetrated against it Computer hackers are sophisticated criminals they are no longer using their basic home computer to assail; alternatively they are now assaulting Internet Domain Name Server system to self-destruct. The duty of domain name server system is software that manipulates the Internet addressing system.

Additionally, the function of domain name is to convert numeric IP addresses that look like 129.206.1.1 into a readable name format like MSNBC.com. Everybody is aware that the criminals have been assailing the local domain servers. The following narration is called spoofing or data identity theft: Hacker mode of operation is to cleverly ask smaller server fake questions combine with fictitious return address in order to reply bogus answer to several and different computers own by people and organization. This situation bears resemblance to a friend who wants to pull a prank hence he/she walks to the pizza parlor then order it anonymously and have it deliver to the friend's house.

Network operators are now apprehensive because the criminal element uses the domain name server software to magnify the intensity of the assaults. Hacker normally dispatch a fictitious question with a misleading return address to a company domain name server, the response is 64 times in maximization than the initial question. As a case in point, in 2003, notorious hacker emptied an attack at Microsoft's domain name servers, were successful in closing down the organization Web sites for three consecutive days. Puzzling as it may, computer relies on trustworthiness of any data input. Computer is like a baby that trusts everybody. Computers generally and honestly believe the return address that is approaching or what computer sees is what computer accepts. One knows that Internet was originally created to satisfy the need of bunch of trustworthy university professors.

Although e-commerce is paramount for providing convenience for both consumers and merchants, whereas several consumers are now apprehensive about security, the concern for their personal dossier being jeopardize when buying commodities and services via the Internet. The vast presence and the competitive low cost of Internet have spawned creativity in e-commerce and its functions. Thereafter society glance several example of what the use e-commerce accomplish, to name few of them, online shopping, banking, tele-banking, television teaching, distance education, online gambling, virtual casino, as well as Pay-TV and video-on-demand services. Companies do benefit from the prospect produced by Internet-based e-commerce.

Current report stated that there has been several sabotage of a renowned Websites that involved theft of credit cards that belongs to vast customers. The major defect affecting e-commerce is security lapses. Customer's privacy is number one security criteria in the world of business transaction via the e-commerce. There is no consumer in this world that would like to participate in any business that would spread his or her personal information/dossier without obtaining permission. Thus, encryption technologies are now the solution that company/online merchandiser uses to preserve customer's privacy. In addition, with confidence many organizations are now depending on security measures provided by encryption algorithms and digital signature, they encourage security of email and electronic payment system. Another one of those solutions for e-commerce security anomalies includes software known as public key infrastructure (PKI). This PKI is a very effective tool that promotes tight security on all e-commerce business segments.

Hacker's operations of spreading dangerous viruses are nemesis to e-commerce. They are noted for assailing networks or e-commerce sites thus they have the capability to close down the electronic services. There is power of defense behind the popular software known as the firewall; that is why several companies adopt the usage of this powerful software. Because of the firewall the security of online business transaction between vendors and consumers are adequate. Online companies are now enjoying the adequate protection from criminal oversight after the installations of systems such as Intrusion Detection System, Virtual Private Network and Information Retrieval System.

Proxy server use by several organizations, though it functions like firewall, this is another security protection that prevents any unlawful intrusion to the internal server even from the external server. Encryption provides technology solutions to the security problems such as converting text or data into cipher text so that interloper cannot read it thus the sender and receiver can peruse the communication. One is now confident of message integrity provided by encryption security and as a matter of fact this software adequately prevents an interloper from modifying confidential information. Thanks to the encryption software, society is now convince that repudiation of messages by online user is now history and can no longer be refuted.

Encryption security is now able to depict the actual computer or identity of the perpetrator transferring the data, file and messages. Authentication and corroboration between the consumer and merchants is now feasible on the e-commerce. Encryption technology is now capable to protects individual confidentiality thus users can rest confident that their dossier are proprietary and cannot be perused by an authorized Internet interloper. The organization where I am employed has policy on Information Technology Security, as it relates to the use of the electronic technology resources. The company has established certain specific criteria for the use of the E: Mail function, including Instant Messaging.

In addition, criteria have been established for the use of the Internet and Intranet, Bulletin Boards and cellular phones, including camera and videophones. The use of Email, Inter and Intranet, Bulletin Boards and cellular phones should be limited to business use with some limited personal use allowed. The policy in my organization is clear which stated that the use of E: Mail for sensitive or secure communications should be limited since it is technologically possible for those with certain skills to access any messages that are sent. In addition, solicitation should not be made through E: Mail except to the extent that the solicitation for an organization sponsored or approved campaign, a holiday project or office event.

Furthermore, the policy states that normally accepted business-related communication in informal, formal formats, informal informational, personal communications, including congratulatory and sympathy messages are permitted. Instant messaging is prohibited. The use of Bulletin Boards is restricted to purposes approved in writing by the management. Downloading, making use have or sending vulgar, harassing or offensive information or have sexually-oriented or explicit material, data or graphics is prohibited. The use of the picture, taking capabilities of computer or cellular phones is prohibited without the express written permission of the management.

My organization may rightfully access and review employee usage of all company-owned electronic technology, including desktop computers, laptops, Black-berry telephones (or cellular phones) and so forth. Computer passwords are to be provided by the Information Systems Division of the Organization's Office or authorized IT personnel in conjunction with the Information Systems staff. Any violation of this policy may result in disciplinary action, up to and including termination of employment, and may also result in prosecution under the provision of any applicable law. The next paragraph will show us the role and process of payment system on e-commerce.

When a consumer is ready to make a purchase, he or she adds the item to the merchant's shopping cart. When the consumer wants to pay for the items in the shopping cart, a secure tunnel through the Internet is created using Secure Sockets Layers (SSL). Using encryption, SSL secures the session during which credit card information will be directed to the merchant and protects the information from interlopers on the Internet. SSL does not authenticate either the merchant or the consumer. The transacting parties have to trust one another. Once the merchant receives the consumer credit card information, the merchant software contacts a clearinghouse. A clearinghouse is a financial intermediary that authenticates credit cards and verifies account balances. The clearinghouse contacts the issuing bank to confirm the account information. Once verified, the issuing bank credits the account of the merchant at the merchant's bank (usually this occurs at night in a batch process). The debit to the consumer account is transmitted to the consumer in a monthly statement.

The process of using digital payment systems or E-count is a revolution in itself hence the steps involve consumer setting up an account with E-count which is popularly funded by a credit debit, and smart cards. The account information is transported through the Web using the security protocol of SSL. After the verification of E-count account balance with the consumer's card issuing bank then shoppers can go on Web shopping spree wherever the credit card or digital payment is accepted. One should be aware that it is the responsibility of E-count to immediately debits the consumer's account and transfer the funds to the merchant. Monthly statements that represent debit on E-count are issue and convey to the purchasers by the consumer's card issuing bank. Shoppers can now enjoy the availability of transaction history provided online directly from E-count. Interestingly, coworkers are now participating in the pay-as-you-ride Smart Card payment system, if they work at an approved downtown location, drive to work and park in a downtown parking lot, or relocate to an approved downtown work location. The Smart Card payment system will provide employees with one daily roundtrip from Metro Park and Ride Lots to approved downtown facilities.

The agreeable solution to the Internet irregularity seems to result in the preponderance of the digital credit card payment systems. Online merchants seems to have rest of minds because of digit credit card payment that now helps to eliminate the problems of no authentication, cancellation of charges, credit card fraud, and on the other hand, the buyers are now confident to use their credit cards. Informal online observer knows that the digital checking payment system is another form of payment system that protects buyers' privacy. There are many attributes allocated to digital checking payment systems, such as faster than traditional checking account, cost effective than credit cards, privacy and prevent consumers information on Web.

The most significant tasks of a digital wallet are: (1) provision of trustworthy payment method from the online shopper to the vendor, (2) validate the authenticity of the online shopper via the use of digital signatures, (3) confidential financial information of consumer are compile and convey to the online merchant. Whereas, the major advantages of digital wallets are: (1) online shopper enjoy simplicity and cheap transaction costs because order requisition is so prompt (2) minimization of fraud and stolen credit cards (3) transaction costs effectiveness, market expansion and branding prospect, (4) effortless customer retention, and (5) smoother conversion of visitors into buyers. Digital cash permit online purchaser to easily and securely make payment to organization or online peers for goods under the amount of $200.

If an online business owner wants to personalize the URL link the excellent process to adopt is to provide guidance through the link that will compel prospective customers to the appropriate page on the online Web site or off-line where the recipient will locate subsequent information about the products and services. However, one finds that the online advertising provides a way for obtaining and understanding customers shopping behavior and interest.

Subsequently, the concept support that business owner can get more prospective shopper to find and visit Web site by using an effective email campaign to disseminate communication such as: brand identity advertisement, domain name advertisement, pop-ups, newsletter, promos, news, e-book advertisement, flyers, business cards and bill board advertisement. Further, business owner should consider incorporating e-mail and Web address on every stationery and assets.

In brief, encourage employee to distribute e-mail and Web address of the company to all relatives, friends and associates. In contrast, if an entrepreneur does not own Web site, the explicit suggestion to act should elicit direction to the off-line business location, or make provision for a telephone or cell phone in order to call for an appointment. Online business owner should be responsible to propagate information about the products or services by utilizing mail services to mail video clip that include business telephone number, fax number, email address, Web site address and street address to all prospective customer, a clear example to follow is AOL. The next paragraph will show us the importance of conspicuousness and Internet marketing basics.

Customers can expect the availability of explicit suggestion to act on the Web site at the front page, center, or end of the explicit suggestion to act as such make it clearly conspicuous. Similarly, a finding supports that a business owner on Web needs call-to-action visibility in order to be profitable. Meanwhile, IBM defines e-commerce in terms of business advantages that go beyond improving process to leveraging the Web to bring together customers, vendors' suppliers, and employees in ways never before possible, and Web-enabling your organization to sell products, improve customer service, and get maximum results from limited resources.

Similarly, the discuss about Internet marketing basics states that business owner must add value to the consumers by eliminating customer desertion, prolong the existence of customer relationship, and adapt merchandises, services and communication to individual customer. Conversely, in order to surmount online sales shortcoming and unresponsiveness, organization should consider showing celebrity pictures communicating about the products or let celebrity wear clothes to diffuse the anomaly. Provide adequate measurement, sizes, description and video clips for all products to acclimatize consumers.

The main consideration for selection of messages should be indispensable benefit of the products or services and dispense the suggestion to the online prospective customers. That being said, the next paragraph will show us the importance of how to treat consumer with simplicity, but before this, specifically, the Table depicted below illustrate how an online business owner incorporated the diverse system of online marketing communications and methods through click-through systems.

Online Marketing Methods	Typical Click-Through Rates
Banner ads	25% - .4%
Interstitials	.2% - .3%
Superstitials	.5% - .7%
Search engine paid inclusion/placement	.3% - .7%
Sponsorships	1.5%
Affiliate relationships	.2% - .5% +
Direct e-mail marketing	1.5% - .8%
Online catalogs	.3% - .6%

The process of obtaining an Internet service is simple, first, by signing a contract, next, by making bill disbursement to the Internet service provider (ISPs). For instance, these are the lists of ISPs: AOL, MSN, Yahoo, Time Warner, Flash-Net, or Billy-Bobs. The ISPs organizations generally control the elements that are essential to business functions of several enterprises. In other words, an access to the Internet generally contains the following elements: (a) a connection contract through DSL modem, (b) service provider contract via cable modem, (c) availability of free email, (d) consistent maintenance of the Web site by ISPs, and (e) provision of speedy connection.
Similarly, your Web site will be hosted somewhere that is already linked to the Internet via a fast connection capable of handling all the traffic your site might reasonably be anticipated to generated. You will utilize your existing ISP

link to upload and download the parts of your Web site hosted on the server provided by your hosting organization. Getting linked via a DSL or cable modem will definitely speed up your work on the Internet, both in using email and in maintaining your Web site, but a faster connection is a superfluity rather than a necessity.

The expenditure is around $250 a year for the faster connection, so make your own choice. Your can effectively utilize the Internet in your business with either connection. However, individuals are now acclimated to the Internet. Meanwhile, the most popular ISPs are AOL, MSN and for the corporate market, MCI. As well, several phone and cable company sometimes do operate as ISP, for example, Version, or Cox communications. These companies have various system of providing Internet access, for instance, Digital Subscriber Line (DSL); this type works over standard copper phones lines. However, other systems provide Internet access by cable model, which normally operate over standard cable lines.

Early in 2001 the domain name authorities (ICANN, the Internet Corporation for Assigned Names and Numbers under license granted by the US Department of Commerce) have ultimately acted to break the dam open. Under the new rules, a whole batch of new top-level domains will be made accessible shortly. Five were validated early in 2001, with more sure to follow soon. As these new domains multiply, you will have broader choices in domain name for your industry. For now, however, I recommend that you register a domain name for your business in the .com domain. Select as simple and clear a name as you can find. If your enterprise name is Lisa' Small and Big, try lisasmallandbig.com or lisasmallandbig.com.

Consequently, a simple and clear name is the frame of reference in selecting a domain name for a business. Since organization are obliged to register a domain name with Internet Service Provider, thus, proactive company should lease a domain name on a standard such as brand identity, keyword presence and recall-ability. There are now hundreds of domain name registrar, that is, organization with which you can register your domain registrars, that is, organizations with which you can register your domain name. Nearly every Web host service provider is also now a registrar. I recommend that you benefit yourself of the registration services of your host service company. Many offer discounted registration services as a (loss-leader) to get new host clients like you.

However, if your organization does much work over the Internet, it is helpful to have a domain name visitors can recall. There are a host of services that permits you to search and register your domain name. Years ago it was very expensive, as much as $100 a year to register a domain name, now you can register a name for as little as $7.95. In addition to having a domain name, it's imperative to recollect your email address will use the domain name, so you don't want something too complex or hard to recall. It's very imperative that the domain is registered to your company's name and not the ISP's or web developer's name, otherwise they lawfully own the domain name. If you ever want to move, they might not give it up. It's also imperative to focus on one domain name and not give out twenty different domain names that you registered for your company, it will just confuse people. Focusing on one domain name will assist in several ways. The goal is to provide the organization with a fully functional system, dependable and reliable, which anyone can rely on. For example, Yahoo offers domain for less than $2 per year and free domain name for the client. A small business owner should independently select a domain name, registered it, the next step is to rent space from a host provider that will offer a cost effective price and handle the technical details. After all, the Host Space provider is a business enterprise designated by the contractual agreement to perform maintenance responsibilities. In any case, an organization renting the Host Space should determine that this particular enterprise carry the following elements such as MS FrontPage, file transfer protocol (FTP) and e-commerce service.

CHAPTER 3
E-Commerce Omnipresence of Money

An online stored value system is a novelty that allows web site customers to make cursory bill payment to online small business owners from the monetary and vital information loaded in an online account. However, online stored value system may only functions after download of a digital wallet. In e-commerce payment systems, the digital accumulating balance systems normally permit customers to buy products on the Internet thus aggrandizing monthly bill payment, however, consumer are not allowed to make installment payment but they must use their checking or credit card account to make full payment. The accumulating balance systems are normally use by consumer to buy products such as intellectual property, products, news, e-book articles, music tracks or chapter of books.

The aggregate of qualities that a business owner utilizes to treat consumers is tantamount to simplicity. This will protect business owner from getting off on tangent. Regardless of the exigency of any company, the first thing to do is to find out what authors or researchers say about current predicament. The archives, books and various article covers every dilemma that confront corporation. What does researcher have to say about how to treat consumer with simplicity? Find out what researchers say and then apply it to the exigency consequently the business email-oriented marketing campaign will become effective. However, in order to elicit trust, construct brochure site with state of the art content, and let celebrity articulate testimonies about organization products or services. Web site should elicit user-friendly and professionalism which is a more positive way of doing business. Accordingly, in order to achieve the desired results, explicit suggestion to act or a call-to-action is always effective when it utilizes simple vocabulary so that prospective customers can easily understand it. Customer is the sovereign king and the reason an entrepreneur is in business, thus, customer always wins every argument. At this point, let us now look into how automated formatting and HTML tags.

To ensure that the customers receive and peruse the email messages in desired format, an online business owner should maintain popular software, the business owner must write and insert email messages in technical acceptable format. Ensure that an element such as font size, line length, word wrapping are legible for online consumer to peruse. Provide interesting content, Web video and audio clips because consumers prefer to have the sense of touch or fondle the products. Let the Web video clips contain people laughing, smiling and providing testimony about the products or services. In addition, online business owner should focus on bestowing free product, gifts and sample to customers.

Several consumers preclude online corporation from sending out the email messages in hypertext markup language (HTML) system because the HTML tags will prevent legibility. Thus, online corporation should utilize plain text to post all email marketing campaign to the recipient. Concurrently, the goals and objectives of the email campaign on the Web site include the facilitation of communications, access and information sharing among its millions of worldwide participants. Meanwhile, the email campaign on the Web site has the potential to enhance consumer access to and use of relevant commerce related information and knowledge. In brief, an effective use of email campaign should result in a more informed, knowledgeable, productive organization and consumers. Having said that, let us peruse the concept of consistency and repetition.

The concept calls upon online business owner to consider insistence of promotional messages. This representation holds that an online business owner should continually post and reveal action-laden messages via the email to the recipients. Consequently, this continual repetition and persistence will compel the prospective customers to consider the email messages emanating from the company. Accordingly, the following are the explicit suggestion to act or call-to-action strategies that business owner can use to convert prospective customers: (a) check it out for 10 days, (b) 4 days deadline to response, (c) free trial with money back guarantee, and (d) free product for immediate response within two days.

The shopper will revisit to conduct another shopping spree from the same Web site because the previous shopping plan experience was fulfilled, consumer obtain satisfaction and every-thing wanted was adequately delivered. An effective marketing campaign is exceptional when online business owner and customer are compatible and understand each other. Accordingly, online business owner should obtain seminar training on how to recognize consumer interest, preference, attributes and behavior. At present, let us now peruse organization performance evaluation and achievements.

The characteristics of a successful email marketing campaign are that the process provides a discipline approach for performance evaluation. One finds that evaluation concept can help company to verify if the effectiveness of marketing campaign is up to standard. Accordingly, online business owner should ensure that written plan is available and implemented outlining responsibilities of company performance. In addition, the company should conduct a periodic audit of the performance evaluation and achievements to evaluate the effectiveness of the email marketing campaign. Meanwhile, the company should incorporate the achievements and audit results to continuously improve the future performances. The online business owner should design annual report on the status of the performance evaluation. Consequently, to ensure that the business owner is consistent with prudent business activities the business owner should establish a policy regarding organization performance evaluation and achievements. At this point, let us look into the feedback mechanism.

Several organizations provide avenues for feedback to be given in order to verify the effectiveness of the email marketing campaign. The record would support the finding that email is the effective medium of email marketing campaign with prospects and customers. In contrast, a business owner should obtain feedback from customers concerning the likes and dislikes about the site attractiveness, product, services, interest, and ask for indication for improvement. The feedback system empowers online business owner to builds genuine customer commitment, relationship and positively reinforces customer retention.

Auto-Router does actually permit the business owner to manage the consumer email responses, conduct timely audits and measure the statistical success of the customer responses for future email campaign. Several scholars demonstrated that the world is full of numerous email response software that online business owner can utilize to verify the total number of the prospective customers responses to email messages. Meanwhile, the target recipient just needs to open the email in order to activate the documentation of the statistic via a response email. However, if emails are preview, but not opened and deleted this situation is not functional for the email response statistics. The online business owner must decide to resolve the lack of response anomaly. In brief, the email response statistic software permits company to understand the attributes, interest and buying behavior of consumers. Certainly, the greater the number of email messages opened, the higher the success of the email campaign.

Digital credit card payment systems advantages includes the propensity to eradicate the anomalies of lack of authentication, customer cancellation of payment, the notorious credit card fraud, identity theft, transaction cost cutting, and producing client confidence to purchase online with credit card. Apparently, digital credit card no longer allows the disclosure of consumer financial information on the multiple websites. The digital checking payment system arrived from the framework of long established checking account and banking enterprises.

There are many benefits associated with digital checking payment system for instance online buyer are not oblige to indicate their bank account information to other party when paying money for the auction, consumers are now free from the fear of uploading significant financial information on the Internet, digital checking payment system are cheaper than credit card for the benefit of online companies, and digital checking payment system are quicker than book checks provided by the banks. The long-established payment systems such as cash, check, credit and debit cards will not work in the digital arena of Internet. As people maximize buying potential on websites the side effect of cash, check, credit, and debit cards might become more obvious. Consequently, organization have now innovated series of digital payment systems to satisfy the demand of the online consumer and merchant.

One thing that is noteworthy about B2C and B2B e-Commerce it possesses different kinds of operation, for instance, B2C e-Commerce marketing system are directed towards individual purchaser that normally make the buying decision. On the other hand, B2B e-Commerce marketing systems are directed towards group decision makers. The brand of a product is responsible for making the merchandise stands out incomparable in the conscience of the shopper; therefore, online merchant should strategize on product quality, reliability, consistency and specialty. A good entrepreneur would build on consumer trust, affection, loyalty and thought process for their product.

In addition, astute marketers should differentiate their products and communicate this difference substantially in the market-space in order to obtain competitive advantage over the competitors. The far-reaching brand strategy involves segmenting the market, targeting different market segments with differentiated products, and positioning products to appeal to the needs of segment customers. For instance, Netflix an Online organization started building its brand by marketing the company services with the strategy of procuring pay-for-performance banner. In addition, customers can take the advantage of free self-addressed stamped mailer for postal returns. In addition, Netflix e-commerce site offers product free trial period and won vast numbers of consumers. Accordingly, the infamous website of Yahoo, MSN, and AOL propagated Netflix advertisement.

Brand equity is the estimated value of the premium customers are willing to pay for using a branded product when compared to unbranded competitors. Consumers are willing to pay more for branded products in part because they reduce consumers' search and decision-making costs. The ability of brands to attain brand equity also provides incentive for firms to build products that serve customer needs better than other products. Moreover, brands also diminish customer acquisition cost and maximizes customer retention. Although some predicted that the Web would lead to (frictionless commerce) and I belief that brands are alive and well on the Web and that consumers are still willing to pay price premiums for differentiated products and services.

Society saw the advent of cost efficient and vast accessibility of the Internet and how it brought into focus a massive ingenuity in electronic commerce and its applications. Several businesses have begun exploiting the opportunities offered by Internet-based e-commerce, and many more are expected to follow. Exemplary applications include online shopping, tele-banking and Internet banking, television teaching and distance education, online gambling, virtual casinos, Pay-TV, and video-on-demand services. Let us now look into marketing and communication online.

The online marketing communication is the system and practices that online entrepreneur employ to stimulate shopper's interest in their products and advertise their brand. Thus, as online entrepreneur want to attract potential purchaser to the Web site therefore marketers need to be knowledgeable about the online marketing procedures. Conversely, the fastest developing channel in consumer marketing is the multi-channel shopper. As matter of fact the lower amounts of expenses incurs from the cost of doing business are major parts of the benefit of marketing, communicating and advertising online. Thus as an example, the cost per purchase for TV was $17, while the cost per purchase for online advertising was $11. In addition to sales, there are vast advantages of marketing and communicating online, which includes progressive brand knowledge of company products. One thing is very important; brand equity would eventually produce sales revenue and profitability. The online merchant also have the benefit to be able to measure precisely the exact amount revenue generated by a definite banners or e-mail messages sent to prospective customers. Although major benefits and advantages of marketing depends online marketing inputs, however, online merchants can maximize their campaign after viewing the effectiveness of online marketing.

The finding is now available that a (low click-through rate) does positively convey the advertisement impact on the consumers because just reading the advertisement is enough to enlist interest even when users fails to directly respond by clicking. Online advertising is now infamous for maximizing brand vast familiarity, understanding, discernment, and consumer propensity to procure. Generally speaking everybody is cost conscious. It is interesting to note that when one compares the cost between traditional mass media marketing and online marketing communications the Web is less costly. What a great benefit, in that accurate revenue is known when online merchant send a specific banners or certain e-mail messages to a potential client.

There are many benefits of marketing and communication; on a global scale it provides people about the detail awareness of online vendors, available products, price tags, quality, and durability. In addition, shoppers can now enjoy freedom of choice; selection, expression and consumers can spend their money for cost efficient product. The reward of marketing and communication are beneficial to marketers and consumers. E-commerce can now boast of reward attributable to vast consumer attraction, buyer targeting, data mining, consumer behavior trail, standardized messages, bilateral communication between marketers and consumers, and rapport between punters and customer services. As matter of fact, this growing Internet usage among the general public, the Internet has already been exerting a significant impact on our society in general, as well as on important disciplines and practices such as communications, marketing, and advertising.

Internet is a new interaction system therefore there is many potential research opportunities to be conducted in the areas of communication, marketing, and advertising. By and large, Internet has stimulated several research theme and prospects to date. Society now understands that the Internet is a proper medium to manage online business for profit, marketing, and advertisement. In 1994, the society saw the reward of the advertisement contract between Hotwire and the AT&T and the commencement of e-commerce in AOL. The global communities have been adequately apprised of how novel and indispensable the Internet is, for example, in the realms of education, communication, marketing and advertising. Let us now peruse Internet marketing technologies.

Internet marketing technologies goal is to dispense guidance, resources, and services subsequently the users need to seize the advantage of and opportunities of today and tomorrow. Internet and ordinary marketing has general resemblance because their main purpose is to accumulate vast consumers in order that the company can maximize its revenue, however, Internet marketing has disparity from ordinary marketing. Internet marketing is also very different from ordinary marketing because Internet marketing technologies now has market-space instead of market place. The Internet marketing technologies is now allowing marketing communication to be conducted at home, work and on a mobile dimension; sky is now the limit of Internet marketing. Internet marketing technologies brought about market-space instead of traditional market place, which is now on a global village. The advent of Internet marketing technologies has spawned convenience at the same time minimizing shopping costs.

Internet marketing interaction is on a global reach thus the world acclimatizes to global customer service. The doctrine of marketing is now reaching hundreds of millions of consumers. The expenses of disseminating the veracity of marketing and receiving response from shopper is minimized the reason being there is one universal standard for Internet. The e-commerce technological aspect of commodities and services personalization and customization for the benefit of customer thus maximizes the ability of marketer to craft brands.

The luxury of video, audio and text does accompany the Internet marketing creed thus it can be combined to bring about richness in consuming experience. The introduction of Internet marketing is allowing consumers to chat thus becoming a co-manufacture of the commodities and services offered for sale. Merchandisers are now busy collecting the consumer financial information and online behavior for marketing research analysis. In order to better serve consumers, Internet marketing technology allows data mining for analysis of consumer data statistics for marketing research.

On balance, the Internet has had three extensive impacts on marketing. The Internet, as a communications medium, has widened the scope of marketing communications-in the aggregate number of people who can be easily reached. Second, the Internet has maximized the richness of marketing communications by combining text, video, and audio content into rich messages. Third, the Internet has greatly enlarged the information strength of the marketplace by providing marketers (and consumers) with unparalleled fine-grained, detailed real-time information about consumers as they transact in the marketplace. Arguably, the Web is richer as a medium than even television (or video) because of the density of messages available, the enormous content accessible on a wide range of subjects, and the ability of users to interactively control the experience.

CHAPTER 4
E-Commerce Security Environment

The Internet precisely permits millions of people to make perfect digital copies of various works – from music to plays, poems, and journal articles – and then to distribute them nearly cost-free to hundreds of millions of Web users. The propagation of innovation has occurred so quickly that few entrepreneurs have stopped to contemplate who owns the patent on a business technique or method their site is using. The spirit of the Web has been so free-wheeling that several entrepreneurs disregard trademark law and registered domain names that could easily be confused with another company's registered trademarks. In short, the Internet has exhibited the potential for destroying customary conceptions and applications of intellectual property law developed over the last two centuries.

Remarkably, there are three different kinds of intellectual property protection law, namely, copyright, patent and trademark. Copyright laws are coded basically to distribute legal defense for the written work of individual such as drawing, articles, books, and computer language program. The law categorically postulated that the work of other people as noted above must not be copied for duration of seventy years. Conversely, copyright law does not offer legal protection for an idea but it may dispense legal defense for an idea written conspicuously in a book, article or instrument. However, the standard of fair use would allow some individual because of special necessity to a minimum extent transgress the copyright law without prior authorization. The advent of the Digital Millennium Copyright Act (DMCA) is here to serve as a significant step to convert the copyright law to the age of World Wide Web. The DMCA spawned a genuine world Intellectual Property Organization Treaty, which made it against the law to make, disseminate or use gadget to override technology that have the legal protection. Thus, anyone who is guilty of copyright transgressions would be fined or sent to penitentiary.

The patent law allocates to the owner of a patent the absolute control of the thought process associated with an invention, and the duration of this authority endures for twenty years. Patents are incredibly dissimilar from copyrights while patents are strong defenses for the ideas but not for expression of an idea. Under processing procedures, the total numbers of requirements that must be met in order for an invention to get patent are four in numbers. The inventor must satisfy the rule of prior arts and practices before patent would be granted. The pioneers did not obtain patent for several inventions that produced Internet and e-commerce. However, in 1990s when the World Wide Web was commercialized several organizations acquired business method and software patents. In the United States, there is always an availability of trademarks protection allocated at the federal and state echelon. Thus, the trademark law protects the community in the marketplace by making sure that people obtain equitable product for what they pay for and desire to receive. In addition, the merchandiser must have spent time, money and effort in conveying the commodities to the market thus the trademark law provide defense to the merchandiser from errors, irregularities and misappropriation.

Trademarks are given to people for the duration of ten consecutive years with infinite renewal. There are procedures laid down for obtaining Federal trademark for example one can get it through interstate commerce or by tendering registration with the United States Patent and Trademark Office (USPTO). Use of a Trademark that creates confusion with existing trademarks is repugnance, this may cause consumers to make market mistakes, or misrepresents the origins of goods and this is tantamount to infringement of the Trademarks rules. Furthermore, one deliberately violates the letter of the law if he/she uses language semantic and symbol in the market arena to wring out money from a lawful owner of the Trademark. Similarly, an entrepreneur should safeguard himself or herself against the Anticybersquatting Consumer Protection Act (ACPA), the law creates civil liabilities for anyone who attempts in bad faith to profit from existing famous or distinctive trademarks by registering an Internet domain name that is identical, confusingly similar, or dilutive of that trademark. Trademark abuse can take many forms on the web. The major behaviors on the Internet that have run afoul of trademark law include cybersquatting, cyber-piracy, meta-tagging, key-wording, linking, and framing. Thus, monitoring controls by regulator are essential to prevent or detect misrepresentation, errors or irregularities.

When an individual completely owns the title to the Harley Davidson motor cycle, one thing is sure, that individual has the prerogative to permit other human being to borrow it. At the same time, the owner may equally exercise prerogative by disallowing other human being from borrowing it. Thus, the same way the owner of a motor cycle has the right and privileges to share or prevent others from borrowing it, interestingly, the owner of the intellectual property have the same protection to share it with whom he or she prefers. Conversely, if the owner of the intellectual property refuses to share it, and if other human being uses the intellectual property, that human being is in violation of the law.

Meanwhile, I want to say that I contend the concept that intellectual property incorporates all the tangible and intangible products of the human mind. As a general rule, in the United States, the creator of intellectual property owns it. For instance, if you individually create an e-commerce site, it belongs entirely to you, and you have private rights to use this property in any lawful way you see fit. But the Internet potentially changes things. Once intellectual works become digital, it becomes problematic to control access, use, distribution, and copying. These are specifically the area that intellectual property seeks to control.

However, the goal of intellectual property law is to balance two competing enthusiasm of the public and the private. The public enthusiasm is served by the formation and distribution of inventions, work of art, music, literature and other forms of intellectual expression. In general, the information technology of the last century from radio and television to CD-ROMs, DVDs and the Internet- have at first tended to weaken the protection provided by intellectual property law. Certain violations of the intellectual property rights should be punishable via criminal enforcement of the law. The judicial systems have the imperative duty to see that intellectual property rights and the Internet contain therein are adequately protected from review, dissemination, distribution, copying, alteration, misuse, unlawful use, mutilation, loss or unlawful removal. We will progress forward by looking into the important factors of privacy and information rights on the Internet.

There are two kinds of threats to individual privacy posed by the Internet: one threat originates in the private sector and concerns how much personal information is accumulated by commercial Web sites and how it will be utilized. A second threat originates in the public sector and concerns how much personal information is collected by federal, state, and local government authorities, and how they use it. Claims to privacy are also involved at the workplace. Millions of employees are subject to several forms of electronic surveillance that in various cases is enhanced by firm intranets and Web technologies. For instance, 76% of U.S. companies screen which Web sites their workers visit and 55% store and review employee e-mail.

Importantly, online consumers should treated with respectable privacy also allocated with information rights to own their confidential information, however, the finding is clear, information technologies violate the privacy of Internet users, because they amass all information without users consent. A citizen may need clarity on the fundamental principle associated with privacy: In order to comprehend the concern related with online privacy one needs to first of all be aware that privacy is the in alienable right of an individual to have the absolute freedom from the derogatory act of surveillance and interference from other entities. Information privacy advocacy group articulated that no information of a citizen should be amassed by any hegemony including the companies or government. Individual are master of their own ship therefore responsible to manage and control the use of their personal information. Due process and fair information practices doctrine advocate for individual informed consent before opt-in/opt-out in other words any information collection campaign should be predicated on permission.

However, the most imperative online privacy legislation to date that was directly influenced by the Federal Trade Commission (FTC), FTC's Fair Information Principles (FIP) principles is the Children's Online Privacy Protection Act (COPPA) (1998), which necessitates Web sites to obtain parental permission before accumulating information on children under 13 years of age. In July 2000, the FTC recommended legislation to Congress to safeguard online consumer privacy from the threat posed by advertising networks. The FTC profiling recommendations substantially strengthen the FIP principles of notification and choice, while also including restraints on information that may be accumulated. Although, the FTC supports industry efforts at self-regulation, it nonetheless recommended legislation to ensure that all Web sites using network advertising and all network advertisers comply. To date, however, congress has not passed such legislation.

The characteristics of e-commerce companies are noted to be in unison when it comes to the activities that threaten consumers' privacy because they are infamous for data, identity, and financial information collections. Law abiding citizen are fed up with anonymous gathering of their personal dossier. The e-commerce companies will use cookie to amass the online consumers' click-stream behavior. Several technological gadgets like search engine, advertising network, cookies, third party cookies, forms, site transaction logs, digital wallet, digital rights management, trusted computing environment and spy-ware are being use on multiple web sites to amass purchasers information and behavior characteristics. One may want to understand the procedures that are in the law book to address online privacy and information rights. For that reason there are Judicial defenses originating from the constitution of the land, Federal, State, and Common laws, including government regulations. At the same time, the e-commerce companies do police itself by having Chief Privacy Officers on their payroll; their responsible includes monitoring for privacy, such as anonymous retailers, secure e-mail, anonymous surfing, cookie managers, disk file-erasing software, policy generators and privacy policy readers.

In the United States, Canada, and Germany, rights to privacy are explicitly granted in, or can be derived from, founding document such as constitutions, as well as in specific statutes. In England and the United States, there is also protection of privacy in the common law, a body of court decisions involving torts have been defined in court decisions involving claims of injury to individual caused by other private parties: intrusion on solitude, public disclosure of private facts, publicity placing a person in a false light, and appropriation of a person's name or likeness (mostly concerning celebrities) for a commercial purpose. In addition, to common law and the constitution, there are both federal laws and state laws that protect individuals against government intrusion and in some cases define privacy rights vis-à-vis private organizations such as financial, educational, and media institutions.

In the United States, the individual rights to participate in online commerce or other without being a victim of privacy and information rights violations is protected under the U.S. constitution, tort law, Federal laws for example the children's Online Privacy Protection Act, the Federal Trade Commission's Fair Information Practice principles, and several state laws. Accordingly, in Europe, the European Commission's Directive on Data Protection has standardized and widened privacy protection in the European Union nations. Industry self-regulation via industry alliances, such as the online Privacy Alliance and the Network Advertising Initiative, that pursues to gain voluntary adherence to industry privacy standard and safe harbors.

Conformity with Fair Information Practices requires that personal information must be: (1) obtained fairly and openly; (2) used only for the original specified purpose; (3) adequate, relevant and not excessive to purpose; (4) accurate and up to date; (5) accessible to the subject for review and correction of inaccuracies; (6) kept secure from unauthorized access or disclosure; and be subject to enforcement mechanisms. Privacy and information rights on the Internet are now responsible for this popular caveat, one usually get from the Internet or e-mail: the mode of operation goes like this, they will articulate that communication is being sent out to particular individuals or groups. In addition, the message may be mistakenly receive by error or collusion; consequently, if the individual is not the proposed recipient, he or she should inform the sender immediately via the return e-mail or permanently delete the copy. That being said, we will now peruse the pros and cons of retailing on the Internet.

The advantage of retailing on-line encompasses profitable operations, higher revenue, efficient production and efficient consumption decisions. On-line retail has become the fastest expanding organization retail segment. According to the prognostication retail segment growth rate will supersede the mail order-telephone order (MOTO) catalog sales channel by the year 2008. Web sites shopping spree has become customary, culture, mainstream and about 75% of Internet users in the United States shop on the World Wide Web. No wonder, consumers are now more confident to buy luxury items such as jewelry, electronics, appliances, gourmet groceries, furniture and wine.

There are many things in favor of retailing on the Internet such as more economically supply chain this is possible because the demand is congregated in one particular Web site, and escalating buyers. Retailing on the Internet has the advantage of obtaining cheap cost of distribution of product because they are parked on the Web sites. Vendors have the capability to amass, serve, and to be a caregiver to great global consumers. Merchandisers have the advantage to cursorily adjust to the dynamic market systems. The online shoppers are becoming more acclimatized to buying on web thus they love to purchase a lot of items of luxury for instance statistics depicts that they prefer jewelry, electronic, gourmet groceries, house furniture, and wine. The consumers are enjoying the advantage of having the virtual information on shopping items like cars, television, computer, appliance, durable and non-durables retail good. The average annual amount of online purchases continues to increase. Specialty retail sites show the most rapid growth in online retail as they develop customized retail goods and customer online configuration of goods.

Online retail achieves increasingly profitable operations through revenue growth and a focus on improving efficiency of operations. The average annual amount of online purchase continues to maximize. Specialty retail sites depict the most rapid growth in online retail as they develop customized retail goods and customer online configuration of goods. Online retailers place an increased importance on offering an improved shopping experience, including ease of navigation and use, and online inventory updates. Online retailers maximize the use of interactive multimedia marketing technologies that exploit the dominance of broadband connections and offer features such as zoom, color switch, product configuration, and virtual simulations of households and businesses. Retail intermediaries strengthen in several areas, including groceries and car, appliance, and furniture dealers. Customized goods, especially in apparel, become financially prosperous and begin to spread to several sites beyond specialty retailers. Online shopping becomes more multi-seasonal and less gift-oriented as customers come to accept the Web as a routine shopping spot that is neither a novelty nor a special occasion marketplace.

There are several incentives of retailing online such as consumer obtaining more financial purchasing power. One finds that amalgamation of demand on one web site causes the supply chain cost to become cheap and affordable. One thing is appreciably known, the cost of distributing product is very cheap compared to the higher cost of the physical store. At this same time, confirmation is present that online retailing got the advantage of being able to sell to overwhelming global consumers. Meanwhile, the vendors enjoy the thought process and goodness of being able to rapidly change the posture of online commodities. Merchandisers appreciate the additional freedom from the expenses of traditional mail and direct marketing costs of catalogs. The profitability accrues to the merchants because they are able to personalize and customize online product offerings. The following are the cons or demerits associated with online retailer, for instance, (1) the vast majority of the shoppers are somewhat afraid of the security protocol of the online business transactions, (2) shoppers are fearful for the privacy of their confidential information parading the multiple Web sites, (3) consumers are apprehensive for the timeliness in delivery of their products, (4) dilemma that ensue when damaged products are return for exchange or refund, and (5) consumer are not entirely reliant on online brand names and probable solutions. There is a lot of confusion when it comes to deciding the preference for particular product from several choices on the Web site.

Time is money, though shoppers suffer from the pain of searching online from page to pages for desirable products without any fruitful selection. The graphic image of the product may take a long time before it is loaded on the computer screen, even if one is using broadband or DSL is no guarantee of less time consumption. Traditional stores price tags may be cheaper and preferable to online. Finally, consumers bear the burden of the shipping cost. However, one whose residence is located in outskirt of the City would normally have difficulty shopping in the traditional stores; thus, online retailing will resolve the distance dilemma.

Online retailing provides variety of products than traditional stores. The technology made it easier for the online users to conduct research on the price, inventory, and the volume in stocks. The dominion and authority resides with the shoppers hence he or she may exercise the prerogative of whether to buy online or in a traditional store. There is always availability and accessibility of Internet: the time is twenty-four hours a day, seven days a week.

CHAPTER 5
Successful Online Businesses

The online financial services stand as prominent multi-channel financial firms. Because of the phenomenon growth, certain sector claim that the prosperity of the industry will continue to endure. This true, the online financial sector is e-commerce exemplary; this is contrary to the bad prognostication at the initial stages of e-commerce. Today, it is the multi-channel established financial firms that are growing rapidly and that have the best prospect for long-term viability. As far as multi-channel function is concerned, it pioneered the lucrative financial firms that are now expanding overwhelmingly and they have the opportunities for enduring developments.

In this modern day, society is now witnessing the significant trend and vigorously expanding financial services. Costumers are now using Internet to conduct research on insurance, finances, stocks, bonds, real estate and employ digital payment system to finalize the purchases. The online financial services brought about the conditions for collection of funds, safeguarding assets, enlargement of assets and transfer of funds. Another frame of reference is that online financial services may be going through mergers but the good thing is that this organization is now providing consumers with the accessibility to benefits, reliance, confidence and faith.

Meanwhile, consumers now have the advantage to buy preferable financial services products via single account at one institution. For example, e-Trade financial corporation is an online financial services that has successfully assisted more than 403 million online customers with financial services programs. However, consumers are reluctant to participate in online financial services because there is panic of inadequate security measures for transference of cogent financial information. In addition, outstanding finding says that online consumers are particularly more afraid of their involvement in financial services transaction but prefers shopping for product on line, interacting and surfing with search engine. Furthermore, costumers are also reluctant to participate in online financial services because of the eminent danger of fraud, identity theft and unlawful access into credit cards or banking account numbers. Several organization have employee assistant program that can help them manage financial crisis, personal as well as work problem. However, using the program should always be voluntary and strictly confidential.

In the meantime, the Internet has constructed the technical base for an online financial supermarket to operate, but for the most part, it has still not arrived. It is not yet possible to get a car loan, obtain a mortgage, receive investment planning advice, and established a pension fund at any single financial institution with one account. Nevertheless, this is the path in which large banking institutions are intending to move. The promise of the Internet in the long term is to move the financial supermarket model on step further by offering a truly personalized, customized, and integrated offering to customers based on a complete understanding of the customer and his or her financial behavior, life cycle status, and unique needs. It will take several years to improve the technical infrastructure, as well as change customer behavior toward a much deeper relationship with online financial services institutions.

There seems to be a movement towards mergers in the travel services business. Reputable companies are buying cost effective online travel services. Established firms currently purchase the weaker and relatively inexpensive online travel group. This is a good thing for the consumers, for the fact that companies intend to develop multi-channel travel sites, traditional stores, television marketing outlets, and websites. Airlines, hotels and auto rental firms are the known suppliers, these industries are yearning to eradicate the intermediaries such as GDSs and travel agencies, and directly deal with consumers. Online travel agencies are very current on the trend of approaching marketers to acquire immense trip inventory after that the traveler buys them, traveling agencies are basically abandoning worldwide distributors and accumulating tremendous revenue.

A casual observer knows that the growth of online travel services with tourism is commendable because it maximizes the standard of living in the United States and contributes $1.1 trillion to the U.S. GDP. Arguably, online travel is one of the most successful B2C e-commerce segments, accounting for more online revenues than any other online category. As the Internet is known worldwide as the popular conduit where consumers peruse and obtain reservations for airline, hotel rooms, rental cars, cruises, and tours. In addition, online travel services are the last resort where consumers bargain for cheaper air ticket. As a matter of fact, online travel services is one of the thriving fortune five hundred online company, a category of business to consumer e-commerce that accrues consistent profit and revenue.

In my organization, according to job description profile, it customary for the workforce to attend several local and outside conventions, seminars, workshops, and meetings to obtain leadership skills or those specific to area of work responsibility. The organization requirement is for the employees to obtain approval for travel expenses, travel advances and the eventual reimbursement of travel expenses incurred. Most importantly, the organizational travel policy delineates procedures for the employees to comply with, as far as booking for airfare, cab fees, and hotel accommodation. In addition, conferences registration fees, airfare and hotel accommodation are often paid well in advance of a trip. Thus, this practice reduces overall travel costs because many conferences and airline offer discount for early payment.

Internet is the avenue normally used by passengers to conduct their research for cheap tickets prices, traveling alternatives, reserve for their air tickets, hotel reservation, rental cars, trip and cruises. Online travel services offer a perfect setting to conduct e-commerce business model.

Travel needs a lot of preparation; information and research therefore people embarking on a journey need the experience of travel services. The public knows that traveling is a product that attunes and works well with digital electronics because to travel, one need to preplan, research, bargain hunt, book reservation and make credit cards payment. The most popular online travel services organizations such as Travelocity.com, Expedia.com have limited numbers of customer services employees that interact on the Web site while working with travelers, thus, customers get cheaper tickets because the organization saves money by limited amount of employees. To some extent, online travel services suffer from the side effect of merging and cutthroat competitions. Intriguingly, the technological advancement brought about the meta-search engines that have the capability to get cheaper prices for the consumer. Thus, revenues are being siphon away from the prominent online travel services companies. Let us now peruse the supply chain management on the Internet.

One may forget to realize that chain simplicity means that company has to minimize the size of a company's supply chain. Thus, the orientations in which chain management, firms and industries organize their buying process are known to be supply chain simplicity. Internet supply chain management normally works together with tactical group of suppliers so that they might minimize the product cost and administrative cost. Internet supply chain management is fond of using the strategy of a long-term contract. Management also delineates in the agreement a major content concerning the outcome of quality product and continuous production. To great extent they promote quality and timeliness objectives. Supply chain management has the responsibilities of bringing together the work process of purchase, production and transporting product from the supplier organization to the purchasing company.

I am aware of the trends in supply chain management (the activities that firms and industries use to coordinate the key players in their procurement process) include: Supply chain simplification, which refers to the decline of the size of a firm's supply chain. Firms today generally desire to work closely with a strategic group of suppliers in order to minimize both product costs and administrative costs. Long-term contract purchase containing pre-specified product quality requirements and pre-specified timing goals have been shown to increase end-product quality and ensure uninterrupted production.

Supply chain management systems, which coordinate and link the activities of suppliers, shippers, and order entry systems to automate the order entry process from start to finish, including the purchases, production, and moving of a product from a supplier to a purchasing firm. Collaborative commerce, which is a direct extension of supply chain management systems as well as supply chain simplification. A manager should utilize digital technologies to ask the supplier and the purchaser to share sensitive company information in order to collaboratively design, develop, build, and manage products throughout their life cycles.

The strength of supply chain management (SCM) system comes from heavily reliance on strategy associated in the system of manufacturing, supply chain simplicity, continuous improvements, ERP systems and uninterrupted inventory replenishment. SCM unceasingly connect the operations of purchasing, manufacturing and transporting raw material or good from supplier to the acquiring firms. In addition, order entry access is available for the consumers as convenient combination to the supply chain management. A good example of order-driven supply chain management system such as Hewlett-Packard (HP), essentially, customers or dealer initiate an order via the Web site and the product are timely delivered to the recipient. Let us now look into the collaborative commerce.

The collaborative commerce is a system of teamwork where the company that supply and the other that purchase exchange occupational functions so that they can efficiently work together to design, develop, build and manage manufacturing commodities. Collaborative commerce is derivable from supply chain system of management; moreover, this system is a paragon that makes supply chain effective. In addition, collaborative commerce is an expansion of supply chain system of management. Amazingly, when an organization seize the opportunity presented by digital technologies, for instance, all party to the association in the spirit of team will work together to design, construct, build and handle products from the onset to the end of their life cycle.

One would find that administration of collaborative commerce permit long lasting relationship between the supply chain companies. Collaborative commerce that normally occur are diverse and responsible to engender several productive activities for example, it may warrant activities ranging from administering supply chain management to manipulating customer or obtaining market feedback to inform employee of the supply firms that is responsible for product design. Adopting collaborative commerce are associated with discharging the responsibilities of cooperative functions with the supply and sales firms, at the same time, functioning as liaison with one large organization through private industrial networks.

This form of collaborative commerce resource are best known for planning, forecasting and replenishment seems to be the one where association participants work together to preplan production, predict demand, manipulate shipping, handle the rigors of warehousing and make provision for replenishment of merchandise. The advantages derivable are eradication of over capacity, lower cost, efficiency and high productivity. Another example of collaborative commerce that comes to mind is called availability of demand chain visibility. Now, this concept permits retailer, supplier and manufacturer to acknowledge the propensity to accrue excess capacity.

The lessons of business network have been appropriated in several organizations, there are no more excess inventories, and in a collaborative commerce oriented organization, high costs have finally become a history. Associations like the one available in a collaborative commerce are free from plague of profit reduction and pressure to discount product price. Lastly, another area of affiliation is marketing coordination and product design. For instance, DaimlerChrysler created a collaborative commerce popularly known as Chrysler Corporation Supply Partner Information Network (SPIN) to serve the vast suppliers amounting to 20, 000 in population. One important benefit attributable to collaborative commerce is the ensued maximization of the whole Chrysler enterprise productivity.

In addition, DaimlerChrysler installed SPIN as a technological extranet that handles the vast arrays of supply chain management and support system. Thus, the 12, 000 supplier employees in a global diverse location do gain access to the extranet to conduct real-time inventory, procurement, demand forecasting, and application strategy manipulations. The part quality supply system contained in the SPIN does manipulate the operations and knows about the manufacturing parts ranging from supplier to shipper, factory installation and after-market substitute. A good requirement for an organization that manufacture a highly engineered part is to get involve in private industrial network or collaborative commerce for the opportunity to manipulate and implement activities like internal design, marketing, quality control, continuous improvement, supplier and distribution partners.

One easy way to accomplish this is to invite the participation of the supplier for instance in design and marketing products. Essentially, one needs to drill the communication of the customers and procure the feedbacks to conduct a research and using the outcome from the research to advice the designer and supplier. Thus, collaborative commerce organizations could be certain that the parts produced by the supplier are actually authentic as claimed. Collaborative commerce has spawned a classical system of freedom of rapport between the suppliers and customers, particularly on partner's forecasts and data replenishment. The partners to the commerce are responsible to deduce unanimous approval to the organizational forecast and plans. Collaborative commerce encouraged the members of the network to access partner technology systems, grant technology empowerment and exchanging information with each other on the Internet.

Auctions are market where the purchaser that offers the highest bid amount will acquire the products. Auctions are market where price tags are changeable and based on the competition among the partakers who are purchasing and selling commodities and services. Auctions can occur between the consumer to consumer (C2C) and also between businesses to consumer (B2C), although one knows that C2C auction are normally associated with a market-space where the sales transaction occurs, for instance, on a consumer-oriented Web site popularly known as eBay, which also conduct auctions for organization purchaser of goods, raw material, inventory, industrial parts and services.

Online portals proffer an incorporated packet of contents and information search services, email, chat, music, downloads, video streaming, news and calendars. One knows that Web portals are the ingress to varieties total numbers of 8 billion Web pages that is now available on the Internet. Society is now cognizance that the function of Web portals is to assist online users to locate indispensable information. However, there is one thing noteworthy, the progress to destination sites offer countless of content ranging from news to entertainment.

Modern portals are indispensable in three areas such as allowing online users to navigate the Web, search content and participate in e-commerce. The category of portal that is most important in the world of technologies includes enterprise portal. Similarly, enterprise portal includes corporations, universities and churches. However, several organizations are now constructing sites to assist their groups and employees to navigate to indispensable content such as corporate agendas, news, announcements and policies. On-line auction and portals are infamous as the focused content portals. On-line portals are sites where one can find well-grounded information on a specific agenda that all online users are interested in. Focused content portals is where one can find the following diverse subject such as sports, news, weather, entertainment, finance, business, boat, horse, or video game. If one wants to comprehend the business models of portals he/she should know that revenue accrue to portals from dissimilar sources. However, online business is currently undergoing a metamorphosis; thus, they are now adjusting to minimization in some revenue segments, especially the revenues derivable from advertising.

On-line auctions and portals actually accrue revenue via ISP services thus customers engage in contract for a monthly fee in order to enjoy surfing on the web and e-mail services. They also produce revenue through general advertising this is done by obtaining a client-company that also pays for advertising rendered. They are known to collects subscription fees whenever they extend premium advertisement services and tenancy deals or transaction for the client-company. Tenancy deal basically means that the client company has a long time or multiple-year contract of being advertised and being position on home pages. On-line merchants normally collect revenue or commission from the web site actively retailing products or services. General-purpose portals want to continue their existence they would create vertical content, attractive or sophisticated site to invites advertisers. In addition, general-purpose portals do have ways to transact business and lure advertisers to their site in order to direct their advertisement to variety of groups. The following are the example of general purpose Portal: (1) AOL (2) Yahoo (3) MSN their mode of operations is to provide solid vertical content channels by so doing a high population are indirectly invited to the portal.

One may want to be aware of the pros of the online auctions, thus the following are the categories of pros: (1) the participants are brought together in a worldwide marketplace (2) there is ample means to find price for non-lucrative products (3) the principle of demand and supply usually craft the competitive price tag (4) the global communities can witness the going prices for the products (5) consumers are emancipated to select product and enjoy higher standard of living (6) the shoppers are delighted for the cheaper price of products and vendors for the cheaper cost of selling. However, the cons of online auctions includes:

(1) Consumers may have to tarry for many days while the auction progresses (2) product are usually not delivered in a timely manner thus extended period of time between purchase and / or delivery increases the probability for errors, fraud or irregularities (3) excessive time are wasted while waiting for bidding and buyers may be frustrated (4) the risks of fraud is elevated because online auction is susceptible to higher fraud (5) the financial responsibilities of packing, shipping and insurance of the product are borne by the consumers. Let us now peruse what an on-line community is.

Online communities is a group of friendly individuals bound together by common interest, they assemble together in a Web site locality to exchanges interest, opinion, idea, suggestion and rapport, at the same time they enjoy collective communication. In addition, an online community is a specified space online where society who belongs to recognizable associations actually rapport together. One thing is paramount to the online community membership, they have secrecy that must not be divulged to the outsiders, and hence, what happen within e-community stays protected. The chief purpose of online community is to attract vast members and to engage in social, educational and political discussion. Amazingly, anybody might speculate about insurmountable odds, regardless of the situation, one can overcome any dilemma that he or she is facing. The key is to join vast group of online communities where one can rapport about any problem thus obtain wisdom, capability and confidence necessary to remove those insurmountable dilemma.

E-Community is the generic name attributed to group of individual who are Internet participants that interact with one and another. The viewpoint or bearing that group partakes in, be it social, political, technology will eventually become the infamous online community name. Another thing that is very common with on-line community is the propensity to carry the name of the function being engaged in, the groups they cater to and the type of technology that propel the community agenda. For example a community might be called high blood pressure support group because this is the type of yearnings that back them up.

The e-community glorify group communication in a diverse environment, one can locate them where they are usually park on the same Web site, for example in the places like chat room, asynchronous environment, Web logs, or Blogs, and one can also find them on the Internet location called Wikis. If one is looking for an excellent avenue to build network with diverse demographics, search no more, because e-communities is the perfect place where one can usually rapport and socialize with individual from different background actually from social, economic, ethnic, race and education realms. Online community offers outstanding information and training opportunity to stakeholders that they will use to lead and manipulate their organization to excellence. Decision makers may also discover ways to respect customers, obtain competences on how to tackle public prospects and quarrels. Let us now look into the digital media.

CHAPTER 6
Customers Retention

The regular American citizens are using more than 3,
900 hours per year enjoying variety of media; this will
probably increase to 4,000 hours by 2008. One knows that
the most popular media are television, radio and the
Internet. However, the three particular media that are
viewed with higher time period are noted as the television,
the next is radio, and finally the Internet. The television is
the highest rated media system thus 80% percent of the
public watch television. Conversely, the finding from the
current research studies propounded that there is
minimization of enthusiasm in watching television and using
Internet more than non-users. Similarly, Internet users have
no interest in perusing books, news, e-books, and magazine.
Digital media are the organization that normally operates in
such areas as television, movie, film and print in order to
interact with the public. This entity also functions in the
business enterprise area of cable, satellite, printers,
broadcasting television, online music, and video rental
stores.

Prior to the widespread of the Internet, copies of
software, books, magazines articles, or films had to be stored
on physical media, such as book, computer disks, floppy
disk, or videotape, creating some impediments to
distribution. Digital media differ from books, periodicals,
and other media in terms of ease of replication,
transmission, and alteration; difficulty in classifying a
software work as a program, book or even music;
compactness – making theft easy; and difficulty in
establishing uniqueness.

According to several findings, television media amass
overwhelming revenue and the next big revenue challengers
in a respective order are entertainment movie, news-books,
educational books, consumer books, magazines, radio, and

eventually the Internet. Digital media normally depicts advertisement thus television and news-book are the media that collect the stupendous revenue from this business model. Consequently, in the year 2006 the net income for the online digital media amounted to $5.8 billion.
Innovatively, the idea of media convergence corresponds to three domains the first is just a technological combination of news-books, television, and radio and stereo component to function as one electronic package device in order to be delivered on the Internet.

Whereas, the second domain, content convergence is the amalgamation of content design, production and distribution for combine operation, finally, third is media industry convergence, is basically the unification of media organizations into mutual operation. In the formative years of e-commerce, several schools of thought were convinced that media convergence would cursorily materialize. But contrary to the expectation early efforts were abortive, and the society now perceives the dawn of media convergence. The following digital media combination that the society are rapidly purchasing or enjoying are PCs, cell phones, PDA, e-book or conventional devices while because of rigorous advertising the print media like news-books and magazine are currently on exodus to the online.

One should be proud to announce that Internet banking is a success in every measure. The purpose of this book is to elucidate about how online banking industries supports sound operational practices, configuration, and management practices. Furthermore, this book will help ascertain if merchant bankers are in compliance with empirical business protocol. In addition, this book will establish if the available resources and technology tools are being utilized as effectively and efficiently as possible. The body of the book will discuss the concepts behind Internet banking logistics, remunerations; article of trade; distribution; pricing strategies; promotional campaign, online security compliance, price and endowment; conditions, findings and recommendations. Let us now look into the logistics of the Internet banking.

The online banking is so lucrative to the extent that Intuit Inc., the parent of QuickBooks, decided to procure the Digital Insight Inc., for the total amount of cash along with debt of $1.35 billion. At the same time, the benefits attributable to this combination are the following: sound financial management, tax software, the ingenuity of QuickBooks, online banking services, timely delivery systems, and vast number of e-banking customers. The Net-bank is the first company located in the United States that eventually inaugurated online banking and in 1996, the Wingspan Company emulated Net-bank. However, the extant traditional banks were essentially innovative in developing the initial telephone banking system but were wrongly hesitant to use online technology prior to 1998. Surprisingly, in 2000, the well-known National bank accrued overwhelming market share because this organization went online when throngs of customers became online banking enthusiasts. Whereas, one finds that about 13 million people perform the following daily online banking transactions, namely, imputing checking, loan, credit card account and paying bill online.

The population of the households that now participates in online banking amount to 40 million; and this is one third of all U.S. household members. Similarly, the numbers will continue to grow; possibly reaching 52 million household members that will bank online. On the other hand, several online banks possess the courtesy of permitting their customers to migrate their money online for free. For instance, the following amenities are seen on the online banking bill payment: (1) To your payees; (2) express payments, (3) make onetime payment, (4) set up a recurring payment, (5) future payments (see, change, or cancel), (6) payment history (including open payments), (7) cancelled payments, (8) add a new payee, see, change or delete payees, (9) payee spending report, (10) report a bill payment problem and (11) make a transfer payment.

Globally, several organizations are constantly busy innovating technologically driven processes to make banking services convenient and available on consumer cell phones.

For instance, a company by the name of Firethorn Holdings LLC allocates the company software for phone installation. Another candidate, Clairmail Inc., seized the advantages of text messages protocol, which are abundantly available on several customers cell phone. Similarly, online-banking software of Corillian Corp is now currently operating on cell phone browser. Society is now aware that the infamous online resources of Corillian Corp now inaugurate the mobile phone banking product. In addition, let us talk about the major achievement of the Chantilly payment technology vendor who has recently migrated data from online banks Web sites on to mobile cell phone. Accordingly, Michael L. Woolfolk Heritage bank demonstrate that the strategy in trend is the yearning to use software to generate revenue and differentiate to business segments from the competitors.

The continuous expansion of profits in online savings accounts has enabled consumers to enjoy e-banking as it usually pays higher yields. Meanwhile, the difference is clear, online banking is not like the extant traditional banks because enrolled customers are treated with bookless statements. They enjoy paying bills online; and make deposits electronically or by traditional snow mail. Another convenient feature is that online customers can withdraw their dollars from drive-through ATM networks. For instance, the prominent Citibank, though an offline bank, has constructed its high yield online savings accounts to prevent massive customer withdrawal of money from their accounts. The net assets of Citibank online saving account have reached geometric proportions of $112.5 billion.

This study observes two core abilities, on one hand is the propensity to financially induce the potential customers and on the other hand is the trend to give monetary incentive to the employees. For instance, there is availability of customers rebate, quality certificate and pay back guarantee that management may use to switch potential customers. The banking industries should be cognizance that employees, at times, perform above and beyond the call of duty and/or consistently maintain a level of performance that distinguishes them from their co-workers. Thus, customer switch incentive program should be designed to recognize and reward employees who have rendered services consistently above average or at an excellent level. The banking industries should place a high value on professional, courteous, caring, customer switching productivity and helpful services to the consumers. Conversely, employees who receive in excess of two confirmed complaints in a quarter should not qualify for customer switch incentive reward during that quarter. Performance incentive is critical element that will ensure organizational goal achievement, productivity and positive result.

The latent customers of online banks are still waiting to be persuaded to become believer, converts and adopt banking online. Thus, blame it on the responsibilities of the merchant bankers who are not diligent enough to persuade the potential consumers. Conversely, one may want to know the debilitating effects of the following factors: (1) as notorious as it is, 35% out of the total segment of banks have online links, furthermore, the web pages are deficient in description of the benefit and advantages of e-banking. (2) Very funny, only one-third of the banking industry engages customers on the operations and services tutorial. (3) Surprisingly, only 35% of the bankers elucidate about the rewards achievable by becoming online banking converts. (4) In 2003, banks still repeated their previous mode of inactive operations. The information on the Web site still remains legacy, intact and had never been altered.

The bill payment is a main priority of several consumers; however, this bothered several schools of thought as to why it was not being glorified on the Web sites. Furthermore, one finds that the bankers were reluctant to explain the bill payment and other services as early as possible to the customers and possible candidates. Given that the bill payment is indispensable to all society, however, the timeliness and reward derivable from online banking innovations were not adequately emphasized to the populace. Accordingly, the Edge Company successfully crafted ACH-based system and now customers pay their bill to small business owners from online bank account, pay dentist, buy ebay auction, and transfer money from coast to coast in the United States, even globally. All credit and power to San Jeev Dheer who pioneered Cash Edge simplifying inter-bank monetary transfer. The ACH system of migrating e-money has made banking industry to achieve the payment technological attainment, further minimizing the business transactional cost. Let us now peruse the price and endowment.

This is a known fact that merchant bankers permit both of the online banking converts and non-converts absolutely free access to their Web sites. Given that several bankers offer bill payment and other services in their individual segment, outstanding dissimilarity, though, were found in the price tag charged for bill payment services. However, fees were taken from the consumer for using bill payment and other services this was common in the period before 2002. Thus, incentives were not provided to the customers who had abundant fund, loan and investment with online bankers. Instead of using bill payment capabilities as an incentive to attract and retain customers the merchant banker did not recognize the market power they had in their arsenal. The year 2003 brought about the percentage increase in inducement of customer with the consideration of free bill payment to all. Nevertheless, 60% percentages of the online bankers are still adamant in collecting fee for bill payment service.

Consequently, the best mode of operation is to empower the management that occupy the higher echelon of organization to handle conversion of customers by influencing the productivity of their employees or customer services through incentives for individual and/or team achievement. Several organizations normally implement an incentive pay program that recognizes employee efficiency and performance by rewarding contributions to each organization goals and objectives.

Meanwhile, organization should establish a mechanism of punishment for deficient or deteriorating performance and provide incentive for future performance and improved productivity. The society is now aware of many recognition programs to acknowledge employee contributions, usually non-cash such as employee awards, recognition, celebration and gifts for a job well done. This can be provided for individual and for teams.

Scholarly community is aware that financial and any incentive encourages customers to adopt a product thereby become an organizational convert. Conversely, the finding is obvious that several bankers refused to use any inducement to stimulate customers to adopt new actions and switch to online banking. Meanwhile, there was a minor progression in 2003 because 4.8 per cent bankers gave non-financial reward to customer that use bill payment. However, in advocating for customers to use bill payment service, 95.2 per cent bankers are against using financial stimulus.

In the same token, the management should work with their workforce to put the incentive plan into implementation. They must establish eligibility criteria for market and performance adjustments. Executive staff's objectives in this area are to establish criteria that focus on high performance with at least three months of customer history with the bankers. Online banking has historically experienced high turnover and/or difficulties in obtaining prospective customers. Incentive atmosphere should have been developed to improve competitiveness in the online market and reduce consumer turnover.

Obtaining and retaining customers represent top priorities for market adjustments. Executive staff should recommend strong emphasis on staff performance and thereby device an employee performance incentive. Banker employees must earn performance awards each year, independent from prior year performance or awards. This should provide a powerful incentive tool for continued strong services delivery and financial performance.

In view of the fact that online banking bill payment process is indispensable thus organization should not make it a secluded alternative but as a primary component of the total online banking services. Correspondingly, all online benefits, namely, fund transfer or email alert should be components of the online banking package. Meanwhile, one needs to simplify online registration process for the benefit of new online converts.

Similarly, organization needs to grant consumers less fatigue activities hence they will yearn to switch to online banking. Organizational effectiveness promotes values when adapting to change, other ways to accomplish effectiveness includes implementing online banking process improvement, projecting cost and efficiency savings, ensuring continuous improvement, quality control and providing staff cross training and development. The next chapter will allow us to peruse the system of circulation.

CHAPTER 7
Online Banking and Financial Services

If several organization is doing it, online banks should not be an exception to the rule therefore management should use several channels to proffer the online bank services. Similarly, online banking exhibition material, presentation and matriculation must be accessible to all stakeholders. The consumers should see where to activate, initiate or conclude an online banking service in a multiple geographical locations thus bankers should make it available on the Web sites; offline; mall, marketplaces, offices, Schools, legacy branch; and on the cell phone. Conversely, given the precedent set by several prominent merchant bankers, it is inconceivable for potential customers to visit a local office in order to conclude the initiation of an online bank account. Let us now peruse the payment strategies.

Online merchant banker should discourage upholding their online services as a self-governing profit center. In addition, banker should proffer inexpensive pricing to entice latent customers to the online banking. For example, customers experience free bank account and all online banking experience with Washington Mutual bank. A bad idea is to encourage merchant bankers to put price tag on bill payment and other services because implementing that ill-conceived decision will prevent customers from conversion. However, merchant banker should know how to craft strategic design that is all-inclusive to attract target customer to sign new account and maintain a lucrative relationship.

Similarly, one would encourage merchant banker to use package of services at one price to benefit customers. Nevertheless, an overzealous pricing policy will eventually discourage customers and disallow them to adopt online channel. Consequently, online business owners can procure their revenue from coast to coast in the United States, even on a global scale when customers purchase products and services.

Meanwhile, an astute observer now finds that, three to four percent of online participants, this is equivalent to 63 million American adults that performed their individual banking transactions via online in December 2005. However, the research community did not notice any substantive progress in 2004. Consequently, the Pew Internet & American Life Project (PIALP) eventually confirmed that flat increases of consumers banking online ensued. This is contrary to the overall maximization of Internet users; PIALP therefore concluded that the society might be suffering from lack of confidence on online banking.

One may positively surmise that the feasible solution to flat increases may be the advent of promotional campaign. The best way for an online organization to utilize its operations to change the future performance is to embark on customer care that is based on providing quality customer service on a daily basis. One thing is clear, the online banking encourages: (1) satisfaction, (2) organizations competitiveness, (3) innovation (4) creativity (5) cheaper cost, (6) convenient (7) modernizes financial products, and (8) lower investment in traditional bank. In a nutshell, one knows that it would be more expedient, and profitable for online organizations to inculcate these benefits into the thought processes of their employees and potential customers.

Online banking does not routinely require the employees to use promotional items to solicit customer conversion on the Internet. Assertively, organization should try all electronic technology and high pace digital media to disseminate their special incentives programs inviting probable consumer to attempt the service. The promotional campaign should use notice board in offline branch to carry announcements, banner ads, posters and flyers. In addition, merchant banker can use e-mail promotions, direct mail, junk mail, and statement inserts. The employees should be given incentive to invite friends and neighbors to sign up. Telephone representatives have the capabilities to enlist a successful convert. In either case, company should distribute a recompense of great reward to employees that successfully and consistently convert customers.

Objectively, management responsibility is to persuade employees to ask consumer to tryout, exhibit usage and facilitate online banking enlistment. Otherwise, the success stories of the banks in Finland should be adopted in the USA. For instance, in Finland potential consumers are normally invited to receive free practical tutorial at the offices of the merchant bankers. Consequently, online merchant bankers should be knowledgeable about the precise worry of diverse segments and use inducement to get people to act now. A good recommendation would be to provide the proper guidance to carry out promotional strategy via all media channel. The management of the online organization should detail comprehensive workforce responsibilities to provide adequate guidance for the control and efficient operation.

The bank industry should embark on sales promotion by beguiling imminent customers to immediately encounter online banking and bill payment. In order to be able to induce prospects to encounter online baking, management must provide pragmatic experiment, incentive, rebate and options that are conducive to various segments. A standing example is Bank of America that has instituted in branch experimentation of online banking and reports about the positive customers enjoyment and revenue enlargement. Meanwhile, the sales promotion method has been quite successful for those banks that provide financial incentives.

Consequently, bankers are hereby encouraged to use monetary inducement to cleverly ask prospective customers to open account and continuous usage of online banking services. Moreover, one should bait customers in order to enhance new habitual characteristics thus online bankers should encourage them to incessantly use bill payment and other services. For example, Citibank invented and implemented financial incentives to stimulate customers to encounter hence get addicted to online banking services.

Furthermore, merchant bankers should craft different aspect of state of the art promotional tools on the online menu contents and acceptance procedures. Consequently, one should enlighten merchant bankers to alter their strategic thought process of products administration in exchange for customer relationship management. Customer driven motivations and satisfactions should be sole focus of online banking business, which is based on providing quality customer service on a daily basis to both internal and external customers.

Organization should grant customers rebate, quality certificate and pay back guarantee in order to build trust, loyalty and customer retention. In order to cover all households, like American Online, online banking industry should mail out free audio and video tutorial program that also contains monetary incentive for successful customer referrer.

Merchant bankers have wrong assumption that the customers are merely persuaded simply by the announcement of online banking services; this is absolutely a wrong thinking that latent consumers are desperate for the online banking sophistication and innovation. In the same token, several organization marketing strategies focuses only on telling the consumer about the availability of the product is enough to warrant the interest of the consumer. For instance, the websites were designed to be functional with little attempt to communicate real values to consumers. In most cases the initial online experience did very little to motivate or inspire customers to utilize the service. Pricing did not help either. Charges for bill payment are common, as several banks follow their traditional cost-plus approach to pricing.

The availability of live customer services to assist customers and the opportunity to aid them in the enrollment process is not entertained. Surprisingly, some organization normally protects or even conceals the telephone numbers of customer service representative. Nevertheless, there are vestiges of banks (for instance, Citibank) have been more assertive in promoting intensive marketing standards, however, the entire industry are wrongly convinced that the society does not need any live customer service call center or persuasions, that customers are yearning to embark on online banking. Meanwhile, some revolutionary banks have taken the leap of leadership and are practicing successful strategies of customer cares, call center, live customer services and persuasions; however, the mainstream of the industry retained the common protocol.

In addition, the majority of the new merchant bankers are following traditional strategies. In sum total, their approach depicts lack of business knowledge of the outstanding issues. The new merchant bankers are yet to decipher the best approach to induce and hasten consumer to enlist in online banking. Conversely, the poignant issues are that the consumer may not comprehend the matchlessness of online process, they don't want to temper with it, and they don't like the price tag, security risk and fraud. Thus, merchant bankers had better device brand new strategies. When the potential customers are not adequately persuaded, consequently, they refuse to become a consumer. To normalize this anomaly management should advance marketing strategies to this group of nonchalant consumer. This strategy can be easily implemented without significant strain on management.

The consumer study depicted many deplorable impediments to speedy switch to online banking, by and large; there is a little growth in the numbers of online banking consumers. However, the customers who are actively involved appreciate the online service. Consequently, the advantages derivable ranges from comfort, timesaving, empowerment and combination of financial services were highly glamorous. In addition, consumers are easily acclimated once becoming active participant thereafter the clarity of the benefits is assimilated.

Meanwhile, the bill payment capabilities are the valuable favorite of the satisfied customers. Though customers were first attracted by common enthusiasm of the online services of bill payment accessibilities and eventually became ardent believers in the doctrine of the online banking systems. The public that is not yet interested in Internet should be cordially invited to banking ground locations where the bankers give them free training.

One can now confidently prognosticate that the imminent customers are bound to equally prefer the benefit of online bill payment. Another thing is certain, encounter, trial and continuous usage of online banking amenities will obviously convince people. Then, merchant bankers should accurately deduce the strategy and bait to favorably induce the forthcoming customers. In order to woo potential customers to acknowledge the inherent conveniences and rewards available in online banking the management may have to consider two diverse methods. These diverse methods are popularly known as traditional communication learning or experiential learning methods.

Research finding postulated that the market is always available for un-haunted innovation, therefore, experiential learning method is highly recommended. The good news is that banks are now tackling the case of nonchalant consumer. Meanwhile, the bank industries should not be advised to use the slow process of communication learning methods because it is inefficient and inadequate to convince imminent customers. For that reason assertive methods should be utilized to induce consumer encounter with online banking services. Accordingly, progressive banks are cost efficient. The vast spending on traditional advertisement should be eliminated. One prominent example is the Bank of American. Thus, online bankers should focus on advancing promotions via experiential learning method.

Online security compliance

In 2003, several bankers were advocating about online aspect of security, one thing common and noticeable is the lip service perpetrated by the bankers therefore; the potential customers remain alert to be persuaded. Interestingly, in the year 2006, the bank regulators of United States promulgated pass-mark's multifactor authentication security requirement. Consequently, the following are the current steps taken by a few members of e-bank industries in order to comply with the online security process: (1) Fauquier bank anticipate to comply with multifactor authentication by having consumers provide their picture, phrase and/or customers personal computer will be registered according to individual location thus the picture and phrase will become the default process. (2) Fauquier says that multifactor authentication for business Internet banking will be in full swing in the month of February 2007, while the Internet banking for customers will be effective in the month of April 2007. Fauquier says that on January 1, 2007 is the time period when general email will be posted to inform consumers to be ready for the update in secure bank e-mail and the banker also anticipate using secure bank email process to inform all the customers in order to minimize the cost of dissemination.

In the same token, (1) MC Bank is now in compliance with multifactor authentication by combining the gadget to Internet banking products. This strong security system works in unison with online banking browser application. (2) MC Bank demonstrated that multifactor authentication for business Internet banking was effective in the month of December 2006. (3) MC Bank gave the customer a brochure with pass-mark security operating manual including a letter about the levels of security. The regulator strongly recommends online banking security performance. Thus, the bank industry should submit it security program criteria recommendation for the review and approval of the regulators. Security reassurance information should be widely publicized to all people through all channels.

CHAPTER 8
Marketing and Communications

The business universe knows that the Opt-ins is an email marketing campaign that depends primarily in obtaining the permission of the prospects and customers. For this reason, the online entrepreneur ought to cross check prospects consent before transmitting email, extend tutorials on how to unsubscribe from the email marketing list and be considerate of recipient computer system by minimizes the bulk mailing. Therefore, when the organization receives the request to unsubscribe, they ought to comply and send confirmation email to the recipient stating that the emails in question went through deactivation from the email-marketing list. This system referred to as option or permission marketing epitomizes the most conservative position on responsible business use of e-mail. One thing is clear business owners should operate under the condition of transparency. Thus, the business owners must be transparent and indicate to the consumers how decently the company will handle email addresses and vital information.

Standard of performance depicts online that entrepreneurs must know the consumers before extending email correspondence. In addition, entrepreneurs on web site must obtain the assurance that email recipients are credible consumers for the products and whatever email list procured by the organization are from authentic and legal source. Meanwhile, to prudently use an opt-out email system an online entrepreneurs must not conceal their identity when sending email, must have the audacity to obey the recipient requisition to terminate email correspondence and promptly comply and not disobey acceptable use policy of (Internet Service Provider) or mail service provider.

The infamous anti-spam activist are noted to use email filter to deactivate and block spam because without this spamming will crowd the computer system, slow down or even destroy the computer system. For instance, the domain names like ISPs and email servers owner does not like online users or businesses that transmit spam, they combat this nemesis by reporting them to Real time Black-hole List (RBL). Thus, spam trafficker will not be able to send email anymore because RBL will block their email functions.

Online users should have the audacity to obey the lawful decorum as a result opposes the act of spreading spam. In particular, the use of Email, Internet, Intranet, and Bulletin Boards should be limited to only propriety business engagement because Spam has become a problem for users of the organizational computer systems. Accordingly, business entrepreneurs should establish certain specific criteria for the use of the Email functions, including Internet, Intranet, and Bulletin Boards.

Further, the use of Email for sensitive or secure communications should be limited since it is technologically possible for those with certain skills to access any messages that are fidgeting on the web. Meanwhile, downloading, expressing or sending vulgar, harassing or offensive information or of sexually oriented or explicit material, data or graphics should be prohibited by all entrepreneurs. In brief, the online organization is required to maintain ESP coverage in order be compliant in U.S.

There are many ways to develop email list, for instance, buying, renting and building email lists. Conversely, to buy an email list it has spam drawback that will eventually destroy the user organization. On the other hand, renting email lists is not discreet because the buyer is not allowed see the actual addresses of the email lists. In brief, the bankruptcy files are full of the online businesses that buy bulk email lists. Again, in email list accumulation, online merchant that follow the easy process will repent and suffer consequences of bankruptcy, but profitable company follow legitimate, hard and conservative ways to procure email list. Overall, society is now cognizance that online merchants that sell bulk email addresses are notorious scammer, spammers and illegitimate business organizations. The cost effective and the best way of building email list are to collect the addresses from the existing customers and credible sphere.

To illustrate, an acceptable ways of accumulating an email list are the following: (1)Via product registration card, (2) Via mail in rebate, (3) Through sales and telemarketing calls, (4) Email sing up list at trade shows booths, (5) Through business conventions and seminars, (6) Long period company build up via Web site signup forms, (7) Prospects and customer contacts based on employee incentive program, and (8) Via warranty and registration forms. In addition, online company uses conservatives, trade shows, parties, word of mouth, employees' families, neighborhood, contest, free dinners and participant sign up strategies to build email list. These authentic email lists are superior and fully in compliance with business decorum for conveying newsletters, sales announcements and weekly sales specials to consumers.

The direct email marketing is identical to post office type of email but the only difference being the fastness of direct email marketing. In addition, the online marketers transmit other kinds of email marketing through promotional content articles that are contained in the email bulletin. All business practitioners concurs that email is a business asset, therefore, a solicitation through email ought to be prudent to the extent that the business practitioners use email solicitations to communicate with authentic prospects and customers. Direct Email are also being use to disseminate special announcement and company ethos to all members of the organization. Some organization use direct email to communicate a token of appreciation, commendation to employees, and to procure inquiries from the key employees.

The piggyback email marketing is all about renting an inexpensive column in the email newsletter so that cost efficient company can use it to dispense product commercials. Society is now aware that resourceful companies are now taking the advantage of piggyback emails to solve problem between online businesses and their customers to advance promotional and customer relations. Piggyback email marketing system of transaction is renting inexpensive column in the email or web newsletter to post advertisement on services or products. Conversely, online entrepreneur can now seize the advantage of email to transmit production capacity to line supervisors' desk, conduct virtual meetings of which the deliberations are archived on the computer hard drive for future usage and schedule employees for daily work. Whereas, an entrepreneur should spread the word in a variety of ways: (1) Submit to Search engines, (2) Pay for Search-Engine placement, (3) Exchange links with other sites, (4) Advertise, (5) Use e-mail (don't SPAM!), (6) Develop a PR strategy, and Use promotions.

One is now cognizance that the viral marketing online is a system where entrepreneur enlist credible customers to spontaneously convey product advertisement and promotional correspondences. In other words, after obtaining customer agreement, company inconspicuously embed product commercials on the email, thereafter; customers transmit the commercials with relations, associates and vast email contacts.

For instance, the free membership of the Hotmail account began in 1995, for this reason, the feature of viral marketing allowed promotional messages to be embedded in the footer of the free Hotmail email account. Meanwhile, this viral marketing enabled organizational promotional activities to be included with the client email messages posted to anyone on a global scale. As a result, online entrepreneurs are now exercising their absolute freedom to embed their promotional messages with either customers or prospects. On the whole, when operating viral marketing capitalist practitioner are better advised to craft and include the following attributes in their promotions: compelling, indispensable, hilarious, enthusiastic and joyful hence the recipient are bound to convey it globally.

When an organization adequately uses an email system, this will allow an effective communications in business sphere, thereby, producing efficiency among work force. As a result, excellent rapport or relations between employees, prospects, and existing customers will enable adequate customer service, enjoyment and satisfaction. In addition, the most benefit of email incorporation includes eradicating barrier and brings connection between employees and vendors. Conversely, employees are more than ever to telecommute or work from home. In brief, online businesses that are using email effectively can boast of order fulfillment and quick shipping delivery.

The society is now familiar with the three different kinds of personal email system, namely: (1) LAN-based client-server systems are based on a local area networks, (2) Internet - based client-server systems, this one allow people to surf on the World Wide Web (3) ASP- based systems are noted for providing Web-based application services. For example, the system expert designed LAN-based client-server systems for organization internal members and they employ it log on, interact mainly on email internally but not externally. LANs has several anomalies, which includes not conducive to email attachment, maintenance is very expensive and highly susceptible to glitches that might liquidate business activities.

The society now employs PC-based personal email system/Internet - based client-server systems to surf the Internet. For instance, there are several client/server company in our society, the following list includes, MS Outlook, Outlook Express, Eudora, Pegasus and Netscape Communicator. Notwithstanding, the following depictions are the benefits attributed to Internet-based email systems: (1) the employees of ISP company repairs the email glitches while business owner only pay subscription. (2) The Internet email is supportive and conducive to attachment. (3) The maintenance of the email servers is the responsibility of the ISP company not business owner and (4) ISP are infamous for extending quality and cost effective services.

On the other hand, application service provider (ASP) is personal email systems that the specialist preferably concocted for larger size organization because they consist of bigger volumes of consumers and prospects. One thing is certain; people are now in recognition that the infamous Exchange Server known as ASP services do belongs to companies like Microsoft, Hotmail and Yahoo mail. In other words, these companies consistently serve their purposes because they offer state of the art email solutions for entrepreneur.

The entrepreneur uses email devices to convey correspondence with few individual. However, the members of company employ mailing lists to transmit more correspondence between vast numbers of groups and subscribers. For example, a list server is an email program that manipulates vast mailing lists. As a result, company that uses mailing lists accrues incredible recompense of great reward. In addition, mailing lists allow company to transport promotional messages to only rightful prospects and consumers.

To repeat, mailing lists allow company to follow rules and provide identification, a working reply-to address and simple avenue for recipient to request removal notification. In short, the mailing list are utilized to distribute information as needed, to encourage discussion group, for example periodicals like e-zines, e-journal and newsletter are distributed to prospects and customers. Conversely, entrepreneur should honor prospects or customers removal request. On the other hand, company ought to peruse ISP or host space provider (the Acceptable Use Policy and the Terms of service Agreement). On the whole, mailing list in comparison to list server possess the power and resources to quickly and spontaneously convey mailing list or email correspondence to millions of people on a global scale.

The appropriate proposal in a workplace is for the upper management to constructs a written email policy and extends that policy in a document to all employees to peruse and be in compliance. Primarily all employees are convinced that their email interactions are private to the participants but the said news is that employers sometimes do eavesdrop or intercept employee email correspondence. In brief, to avoid divided interest employees should use their personal email when they reach home because workplace is a place where worker do discharge duties and timely completion of job assignment is the essence of business.

Entrepreneurs that have vast employees on the payroll yearn for appropriate kind of network. Consequently, large company will do better by choosing the virtual private networks (VPN). Similarly, with VPN there is availability of collaboration between distant companies in different geographical locations. Moreover, VPN allow company to connect to Internet with adequate data security. Further more, VPN contain modern computers that encrypt and decrypt all the information that go back and forth on the Internet. In short, VPN can boast of tight security, internal controls and cost effectiveness.

When one think about improving business operation Internet technology probably is the answer. For instance, there are many advantages of having Web site in your organization which includes production of increase in the level of operation, cost efficiency, lower cost of printing, greater productivity, customers satisfaction and email/communication improvement. Similarly, companies now have the privileges to migrate forms document onto the Web site in either PDF file or html. For example, employee, prospects and customer can peruse, download or print the following items from the Web site: company mission, company culture, employee insurance forms, policies and procedures, job application, and customer order forms.

Online businesses ought to find an avenue to bring satisfaction and contentment to their customers. In other words, the management can adjust inventories capacities and employee work schedule to spontaneously meet the specific needs of customers. For example, the customers deserve extra support services that all online users prefer. Similarly, online business management ought to immediately provide response to customers' questions, more thoroughly and more personally. One knows that it is the duties of a company to find out what customers are buying so that they can adequately make their inventory more conducive and responsive to consumers need.

A good idea to know that organizations are now figuring out when their customers shop, so that staff schedule can be adjusted, store hours changed, and workforce are then available when they are needed. In addition, companies ought to learn more about consumers in order to treat them in a friendly manner by calling them by their first name, know customers friends/families, and know customers preferences. Thereafter adjust company production, services, selection, and correct the weak spots in efficiency. Conclusively, online businesses are now infamous for using web-based customer service to better serve customers as a result.

The business etiquette will have us believe that in order to make online shopping experience hilarious, accommodative and grow consumers the management of a company should craft a user friendly online. Conversely, no wonder online users are reluctant shop online because of the poor visibility and reputation of some organization. Entrepreneur should have the respect and audacity to obey business concept to design a solid introduction about the online business. Similarly, a general description of the online company and the line items is adequate to induce and encourage potential consumers to switch to online shopping spree. Moreover, the following lists will stimulate consumers to purchase online: (1) Display the name of the CEO/Owner/President/Manager with big font on the online front page (2) Portrays organization history on the front page (3) Depict 24/4 telephone, cell and fax numbers (4) Portray satisfied customers commentary.

The online consumers seeks legitimacy assurances from the online business entrepreneur, therefore, the business upper echelon ought to post the twenty four hours telephone number of the company key contact on the Web page. As a result, the confidence level of the potential customers will increase tremendously. Most importantly, there is no need to hide the identity of the personnel, thus, company that yearn for profitability should get out the closet and conduct the online business with full transparency.

As customers must rightly have a precise understanding of the product, that company sells and the way organization fit into grand scheme. Similarly, companies ought to give consumers instructions programs about the price tags of their purchases. One might want to tell the retail customers why they are paying higher amount for a single item than wholesale customers pay for theirs on a per item basis. One thing is clear, both prospects and customers normally prefer business transparency and full disclosure.

In the aspect of industry overview of businesses, one finds that organizations normally attach links to their business allies. Meanwhile, online companies associates with complementary businesses are now infamous for embedding reciprocal links directing their visitors back to each other Web site. Consequently, this kind of collaboration between industries does produce substantial privileges to all participants with no comparison in the offline world. For example, an auto repair shop that engages in import might collaborate with a Radiator repair shop, Auto parts stores, Auto body shop, Tire store, used car sales and Vehicle Inspection station.

The online front page is the area where online businesses depict the products and services offered for consumer consumption. At the same time, online businesses have the responsibility to construct a unique product story or unique selling proposition (USP). Hence, the product pages in company Web site must be very explicit on company's unique product story. Meanwhile, companies ought to focus on USP point, for instance, selling point to the customer should include: this company offer free delivery, extended warranty, large product selection, knowledgeable sales people and the most expert service personnel. In brief, to prudently decipher activity of a company that focuses on USP-based, the findings will probably be that of embedding it on the header or footer of their web site. By the way, the footer should carry the name and contact information of the Webmaster.

CHAPTER 9
Market Opportunity Analysis

The online surfers click directs them to the first page of the Web site and this correspond to the Home Page. Meanwhile, people sometimes call it entry page to the Web site. The main purpose of the Entry or Home Page is to extend a good initial impression on visitors. Similarly, Home Pages are normally being employ to emphasize to online users whose site they are visiting. In addition, Home Page permits easy access to interior pages that are available on the Web site. Conversely, the Home Page blocks visitors from spontaneously viewing a list of all the files in a particular Web server directory.

Any one intending to do business online should not be too much preoccupied with the nemesis of security risks because any one that want to obtain a gold from the rocky mountain will not look at the edge of the utensil. There is no need to daydream, get involved and start your profitable enterprise on the Web. Nevertheless, the long arm of the law is the current remedy against Hacker that attack personal computer and Web site. Meanwhile, to guard against damages or loss of online business data through accident or deliberate act for this reason an entrepreneur should implement a daily duplication of data and systematic backup of the indispensable business data. In short, the company safeguard copies of the duplicated data and the systematic backups in a remote location for adequate protection from fire disaster.

The online ordering is right for any organization that wants to seize the advantages of the global consumers predicated on the habitual tendency of online purchase. On the other hand, customers on a global scale desire to buy at a distance because they do not have the luxury and availability of the products in their geographical locations. One thing is abundantly clear; there is a need, smart entrepreneur had better satisfy needs of the consumers.

Most money in e-commerce is made by selling products either physical or digital. Many of the same common sense rules apply whether you are selling products online or offline. As an entrepreneur you should anticipate to sell products with high margins, high demand, low competition, etc. Many businesses sell services on the Internet. Some examples include Web hosting, domain name registration, hosted software applications, and comparison-shopping services.

A new entrepreneur that wants to craft online newsletters for subscription must walk the road carefully because the online businesses of this segment have seen countless demise and investors have lost tremendous funds. In contrast, Wall Street journal and Business Tech are the only online subscription based magazine that are still functioning, however, the rest of this kind of online segment began as online subscription but went back free access because of lack of patrons and consumers refusal to pay for access. Whereas, the following side effects are the criterion that prevented consumers from purchasing online subscription: (1) Any publication that is of general interest (2) Lack of economic reasons and (3) No print publication. In general, people will pay to access online publication if it has electronic version, they will patronize if there is financial reward and no alternative.

Another use for business Web site is to deliver the products directly to the customer's computer hard drive. Obviously, this application has some severe limitations: the product you as an entrepreneur is delivering must be electronic in nature. The obvious example is computer software. Note, however, that there really are a number of other items that practically any business can deliver to customers from a Web site. Here are a few possibilities:
    (1) Reports your usually sell in print form.
    (2) User manuals for the gadgets you sell, including those
        for obsolete gadgets
    (3) How-to manuals for the components you sell
    (4) Project plans for the components you sell

(5) Pictures or other graphic art to be used in customers' commercial applications

(6) Audio or video clips to be use in customers' commercial applications

(7) Your musical compositions for sale directly to individuals

(8) Your self-published stories and books

(9) Stories and books you publish for others.

(10) Cartoons and comic strips you create for sale

(11) Resumes, pictures, and bios for your clients, if you are a headhunter

(12) Newsletter you sell or provide for free that are designed to be printed and distributed by your commercial customers.

(13) Press releases

Any time you can find a way to deliver your products-even part of them effectively in an electronic format using your Web site as the source, you are almost confident to save money over any other method you might consider. ASP is one of the services where consumers avoids downloading and install software instead indulge in using application that is available on the Web sites, for instance, to prepare income tax and filed the same returns right on the Web Site. Another use for business Web site is to convey the product you sell directly to the customer's computer hard drive. Obviously, this application has some severe limitations: the product you are sending must be electronic in nature, the evident example is computer software.

The broadband Internet has the speed that can really enable business to conduct project as fast as possible. Accordingly, anyone that transmits promotional mailing through email may be able to get result as soon as possible. Online merchants should avoid being tardy in conducting project because punctuality is the essence of an enterprise. Thus, business owners should avoid procrastinating project but must initially use learning process project that are always quickly accomplish before proceeding to complex projects. On the contrary, just as in an offline business, an entrepreneur will have to figure out how to make money. It will help if an entrepreneur create a business plan, and consider what other successful online businesses are doing. Some options include: (1) Extend your existing (brick-and-mortar) business online, (2) Sell products, (3) Sell services, (4) Sell information, (5) Sell advertising, (6) Become a reseller.

As long as owners of online businesses thought processes are that of responsibility, fortitude and in absolute control of any project or endeavor, an entrepreneur circumstances will bow their knees to simplicity. Online business is not so different from any other sort of start-up undertaking; the same principles apply. Think about what makes an offline business successful, and then scrutinize your Web business in the same way.

There is never adequate money to go around in the typical small business. Over the years, I have learned from my business customers that most projects costing a lot of money will never materialize. The systems recommended here are organized to scale from very low-cost, entry-level systems to more expensive, custom systems. In every case where investment fund is at a premium, I recommend that the first effort be addressed as a proof-of-concept trial. Most of the suggestions cost practically nothing to try. In fact, many do not cost much even when scaled up. If you keep your proof-of-concept trial projects simple, they will also be inexpensive.

Marketing efforts will reveal you to business risks that are exclusive to the Internet in addition to the general business risks you already run in the ordinary course of your business. As a successful business professional, you probably are already pretty good at appraising the quality of the advice you get. You will make up your own mind about what you are reading in this book, for example. If a hammer does a good job of driving nails, it is also very effective at bashing in somebody's head. If a knife is effectual at slicing vegetables, it is also probably effectual at well, you get the picture. If people cannot effectively use a technology application for harm, it probably will not be effective for business use, either. Stated another way, effective tools can be dangerous weapons when misused by people.

An entrepreneur should become an affiliate, an affiliate accrues funds by sending buyers to another merchant's web site. The merchant pays the affiliate either a flat fee per sale or a percentage of sales originating from the affiliate. To succeed you will need competent professional in search engine marketing or a web site that already attracts a lot of traffic. Affiliate models entail little up-front financial investment and no inventory. However, you will need to produce a lot of traffic to accrue finances in affiliate marketing because revenues per sale are generally low.

Be belligerent in your use of the Internet and conservative in the design of your legal organization. If you adopt a belligerent approach to the use of the Internet for marketing, let's say you elect to send obvious spam, your existing business could be irreparably harmed. To help avert damage to your existing business, my suggestion is that you create a new legal entity, a corporation or an LLC (limited liability) which you isolate your aggressive marketing tactics. Keep your current business out of it entirely.

Of course, if you comply with my advice you are not going to engage in obvious spam, are you? Even so, and even if you are very cautious about which customers and prospects you choose to send promotional messages to, given the volatile and uncertain legal atmosphere surrounding the business uses of the Internet, the risks are still quite high. Do yourself a big favor. Spend the 100-to-500 bucks it takes to develop a separate legal entity under which you can accomplish all your Internet marketing tactics.

In addition to implementing a separate legal entity under which you can more safely practice your online trade, I also recommend that you seek legal advice before implementing any e-business strategy of consequence. Make sure the attorney you employ is specifically knowledgeable in Internet law, and is not just some attorney who has a Web site.

The personal email is the best tools or apparatus for medium entrepreneur to embark on when conveying promotions, newsletters to prospects or customers. The list management tool like (ListMate) helps online business owners to implement removal request, handle vast email client, and address list. An entrepreneur can use free mailing list or email-based mailing list to conduct mailing list marketing. Society is now aware that University, non-profit organization, and discussion group uses the following mailing list servers like: Majormo, LISTSERV, and List Proc.

A new business entity may get permission and join the server of Majormo, LISTSERV, or List Proc. Having accomplished admittance to the server of the organization the new business will get exposed to vast mailing lists. The mailing list marketing starts with accumulating email address list, entrepreneur can accrue this list from newsletters, promotions, discussion groups and subscriptions. Entrepreneur may procure from vendors' free mailing lists, fee based ASP mailing lists or rent a list but they should guard against scammer or spammer nemesis. In addition, entrepreneur should crosscheck their identification, references and their IP address against that one available in the coffer of RBL (Real-time Black-hole List) at www.maps.vix.com.

Email is a method of electronic communication both internally and externally to correspond with user groups, prospects, customers, newsletters and discussion groups. The online company follows set of protocol when they procure email address list from newsletters and discussion groups. For instance, an acceptable ways of accumulating an email list are the following:

(1) Via product registration card
(2) Via mail in rebate
(3) Through sales and telemarketing calls
(4) Email sing up list at trade shows booths
(5) Through business conventions and seminars
(6) Long period company build up via Web site signup forms

(7) Prospects and customer contacts based on employee incentive program

(8) Via warranty and registration forms.

The authentic email lists collection process noted above does comply with business decorum of authorized consent. Meanwhile, this kind of acquired email lists is then appropriate for conveying newsletters, sales announcements and weekly sales specials to the global consumers. Email correspondence is an asset that primarily help an online organizations to accumulate potential address list, otherwise, online organization can rent, buy or build email address lists. In brief, an online organization uses email addresses to conduct products or services promotional advertisement.

Mailing list-promos, newsletters, and discussion groups-each require specific procedures. Working from the simplest to the most complex, the procedures required in each of these three applications are shown in this book. Business owners should execute these steps in managing promos: (1) determine the purpose of the promo and set concrete goals for results. (2) Establish a system for monitoring results, (3) devise a distribution plan for your promotional messages. (4) Devise a plan for managing mailing list(s), (4) Create messages to be delivered (as needed), (5) Deliver messages (as per plan), (6) Handle responses as per plan, and (7) Post results to planning tool and evaluate performance per plan.

Entrepreneurs should implement the following steps to manage newsletters: (1) determine the purpose of the newsletter and set concrete goals for results. (2) Establish a system for monitoring results. (3) Devise a plan for acquiring addresses to add to your distribution list. (4) Devise a plan for managing mailing list(s). (5) Create messages to be delivered (as needed). (6) Deliver messages (periodically as per plan). (7) Handle responses as per plan (as needed throughout the day). (8) Post results to planning tool and evaluate performance (daily).

One should define the purpose of the discussion list and write an introductory memo to be sent to new customers. Choose an apt mailing list system and determine the methods you will utilize in that system to perform the following routine tasks: (1) Import lists of subscribers to be added. (2) Add individual new subscribers. (3) Remove individual subscribers. (4) Remove lists of subscribers. (5) Moderate messages from members. (6) Produce a daily digest of posted messages that can be sent as an option in place of sending individual messages separately. (7) Send messages to the list. (8) Archive posted messages.

Construct an apt email footer to be included in all your postings to the list and organize your mailing list systems to include your footer. Determine the methods (s) to be utilized to solicit new members and implement those methods. Entrepreneurs should implement the following: (1) Review incoming messages and post approved messages to the list (as needed through out the day). (2) Post your own messages to the list (as needed throughout the day), (3) Accumulate posted messages into the daily digest (end of day), (4) Add subscribers to the member list (end of day), (5) Remove from the member list those requesting to be unsubscribed (end of day), (6) Post the daily digest to the members requesting the digest option (end of day), and (7) Archive posted messages (as needed: weekly or monthly).

Online organization should clearly establish, articulate and employ goals and objectives to maximize performance standard of mailing list application. Ensure a written goal or plan to accomplish by using the mailing list is developed and implemented. Organization members will be responsible for consistently applying and enforcing goals and objectives, and promptly review facts and circumstances surrounding deviations from the standard of operations. No matter what your business purpose in utilizing a mailing list, the place to commence is to determine what you wish to achieve by using the mailing list and then set some concrete criteria and goals for your efforts.

Adopting the right policies pertaining to all of your mailing list activities will assist you get the result you want while greatly minimizing the probability of generating a negative reaction to your mailing list activities. Your two most imperative policies deal with the technique you use to accumulate prospecting addresses and the way in which you manipulate your list. Managing a new letter or group discussion list is comparatively simple and straightforward. You add the addresses of new subscribers and obliterate addresses of those who wish to unsubscribe. With promos, because recipients do not subscribe to your list, managing address lists includes verifying addresses as well as managing remove requests.

CHAPTER 10
Viral Marketing Concepts

Once you have an address list and a system for manipulating the list so that your messages go to the right group of customers, your next challenges will be deciding how often to convey messages and constructing messages that get the results you are after. How often to direct email to your list depends on a lot of variables: whether it is a discussion group a newsletter, or a promo, as well as what your prospective costumers' want, what you are able to provide them, and countless other factors we will never be able to quantity, let alone control. In general, you will need to test the impacts of mailing frequency on your goals. Even though I cannot offer you tangible mailing schedules, some observations are plausible for each type of mailing list you adopt in your business.

The purpose of most mailing activities you accept in your business will be to produce a positive reaction. For example, one might want the recipient of email communication to: (1) Navigate your Web site. (2) Call you for more facts or to place an order by phone. (3) Purchase right from the email message with a reply message. (4) Contribute to your newsletter by sending a reply. (5) Take one of many other possible actions. Just address in the usual manner any responses you get that are analogous to those for which you already have a system in place. A phone call is a phone call, and you should already be surveying the callers to determine what made them call. In addition to the responses you want, you will also receive responses you do not want, such as flames (irate messages) from irritated recipients, bounced messages, and remove requests. No matter what the responses from your mailings, deal with every one of them immediately. Do not get slack here. Failure to answer within a few minutes to an order question can result in losing the order to another online competitor. A quick and humble response to a flame from an anti-spam vigilante can instantly defuse what could rapidly turn into a raging disaster if ignored for even a few hours. All of the messages you get need to have a categorization and a place where they belong. Just read what you need to decide how to categorize the message, then deal with it and move on.

Online small business owners are responsible for providing performance guideline for mailing list and shall have the responsibility of ensuring compliance with the guideline. Thus, online merchandiser should assess mailing list supporting systems to determine the performance evaluation of the mailing list. Meanwhile, the report must be issued that shall also identify the controls that were evaluated, the controls that were not evaluated together with the reasons why, and the material weaknesses identified because of the evaluation. Similarly, the operational manager must issue compliance report or a statement of positive assurance with respect to those items tested for compliance, including compliance with performance guideline pertaining to control reports. In brief, the report should include negative assurance on those items not tested, and a summary of all instances of noncompliance.

Society is now cognizant that the viral marketing online system is immensely cost effective, no cost sustain on marketing, and transmittable. The viral marketing enables dissemination of websites commercial and product contents to vast online users on a global scale. Viral marketing is a system whereby entrepreneur enlisted customers spontaneously to convey product advertisement via promotional correspondences that are inconspicuously attached in their email communication with relations, associates and vast email contacts.

The free membership of society in the Hotmail account began in 1995, thus, online businesses seized the advantages of viral marketing by embedding promotional messages in the footer of the free Hotmail email account. In other words, organizational promotional activities are included when correspondence are sent by a Hotmail client to anyone on a global scale. Online entrepreneurs are now exercising their absolute free to embed their promotional communications with either customers or prospects. When operating viral marketing capitalist are better advised to craft and include the following attributes in their promotions; compelling, indispensable, hilarious, enthusiastic and joyful hence the recipient are bound to convey it to any extent.

The society is now familiar with the three different kinds of personal email system, namely: (1) LAN-based client-server systems infamous for being based on a local area networks, (2) Internet - based client-server systems, this one allow people to surf on the world wide web (3) ASP-based systems are noted for providing Web-based application services. The system expert designed LAN-based client-server systems for organization internal members thus work force employ it log on their computers, interact mainly on email internally but not externally. LANs has several anomalies, for instance, LAN is not conducive to email attachment, maintenance is very expensive, and highly susceptible to glitches that might liquidate business activities.

Application service provider (ASP) is personal email systems that the specialist preferably created for larger size organization because they comprise of bigger volumes of consumers and prospects. People are now in acknowledgement that the infamous Exchange Server known as ASP services do belongs to companies like Microsoft, Hotmail and Yahoo mail. These companies constantly offer state of the art email solutions for entrepreneur. Online users normally utilize PC-based personal email system or Internet - based client-server systems to surf the Internet. The major service providers include Internet Service Provider (ISP) or Broadband.

There are several client/server company in the western world, the following list includes, MS Outlook, Outlook Express, Eudora, Pegasus and Netscape Communicator. The following depictions are the benefits attributed to PC-based or Internet-based email systems:

(1) The employees of ISP Company overhauls the email glitches while business owner only pay subscription.

(2) The Internet email is supportive and conducive to attachment.

(3) The maintenance of the email servers are the responsibility of the ISP company not business owner.

(4) ISP is infamous for extending quality and cost effective services.

The entrepreneur uses personal email devices to convey correspondence with few individual. However, the members of larger company employ mailing lists to transmit more correspondence between vast numbers of groups and subscribers. For instance, List Server manipulates vast mailing lists. Meanwhile, Companies that employ mailing lists are always the recipients of recompense of great reward. Furthermore, List Server facilitates company to transport promotional messages to only rightful prospects and consumers. To illustrate, List Server enables company to comply with online policies, provide identification, a working reply-to address and simple avenue for recipient to request removal notification. In brief, the mailing list are utilize to distribute information as needed, to encourage discussion group, for example periodicals like e-zines, e-journal and newsletter are distributed to prospects and customers.

Entrepreneur should honor prospects or customers removal request and peruse ISP or host space provider (the Acceptable Use Policy and the Terms of service Agreement). To illustrate, the List Server receives correspondence address to a noted mailing list; the staff thereafter disseminates the messages to every single address in the email list applicable with that noted mailing list. In addition, the list server actively manipulate each separate mailing list by performing subscribe and unsubscribe functionality these are done because list servers are recipient of the request from the email. Consequently, the act of employing mailing list in comparison to list server engender the power, resources, and to quickly spontaneously convey email correspondence to millions of people on a global scale.

Entrepreneurs that have vast employees needs appropriate kind of network. For example, the virtual private networks (VPN) allow company to connect to Internet with adequate data security. Similarly, VPN contains modern computers that encrypt and decrypt all the information that go back and forth on the Internet. Accordingly, VPNs can boast of tight security internal controls and cost effectiveness. In brief, with VPNs there is availability of collaboration between distant companies in different geographical locations.

The concepts of web-based customer services propounds that entrepreneur should escalates customer relationship, gratification and enjoyment. Thus, this concept states that company should make sure that consumer are the boss. The concept of web-based customer service encourages company to solve customer emotional needs, treat customer well, and prudently insert cordial rapports to customers via email correspondence. Company should comment that each employee is responsible for their own behavior when it comes to chatting about subjects that may encourage, compliment, and service consumers. When it comes to meeting the needs of the consumers, it all comes down to respect, that is respect for self and more importantly respect for consumers.

Sensitivity is the essence of customer service. They are aware of the issue of not enough memory space on personal computer of customers; thus, some company went above the call of responsibility and found solution. For example, instead of customer downloading and installing software, Turbo Tax has now embedded on www.quicken.com/taxes Web site. Customers are now enjoying the time saving and convenience by visiting quicken site, prepare their tax return on Web pages, thereafter, and file the tax return on the same Web pages. Online users are now enjoying the concepts of web-based customer services via mortgage calculators; haircut schedule, Auto repair appointment and payments schedule are now available on the Web site.

To choose the right tools for mailing list marketing

The personal email is the best tools or apparatus for a medium entrepreneur to embark on when conveying promotions, newsletters to prospects or customers. The list management tool like (ListMate) helps online business owners to implement removal request, handle vast email client, and address list. An entrepreneur can use free mailing list or email-based mailing list to conduct mailing list marketing. Society is now aware that the University and nonprofit organization like discussion group employ the Majormo, LISTSERV, and List Proc servers for the mailing list marketing activities.

A new business entity may get permission and join the server of Majormo, LISTSERV, or List Proc. As a result, the new business will enjoy to vast mailing lists marketing and profitability. The mailing list marketing starts with accumulating email address list, entrepreneur can accrue this list from newsletters, promotions, discussion groups and subscriptions. Entrepreneur may procure from vendors' free mailing lists, fee based ASP mailing lists or rent a list, nevertheless, they should guard against the nemesis of scammer or spammer. In addition, entrepreneur should crosscheck the identification, references and their IP address against that one available in the coffer of RBL (Real-time Black-hole List) at www.maps.vix.com.

To procure a domain name registration an entrepreneur need to consult domain name registrar. They usually select the domain and when there is tendency to register the domain, the proper thing is to accomplish it via the service provider. Accordingly, the responsibility of the service provider includes solving computer technicality. In brief, entrepreneur needs to choose a host service provider that is inexpensive and knowledgeable about the line of business.

A responsible email targeting would include emotional pitch, solve customer need and rigidly worded to emphasize the word of the product advertisement. Online entrepreneur should use every communication skill to elicit trust, eliminate emotional dilemma, finally induce and motivate a potential customer. One will note that online users would gladly surrender their personal information when they are convinced that your enterprise possesses exclusive product to proffer. Online entrepreneur should have customer service employees knowledgeable of the business to provide information, ease the novices of online users, encourage and personalize messages. The society conceded that the responsible email targeting is compliant with the policies, laws and predicated on obtaining consent with clear agreement of the recipients.

Entrepreneur essential functions include procurement of vital information of the prospects and customers before forwarding any email. In addition, entrepreneur must be certain that all recipient are latent customers for their merchandise. Meanwhile, the online business is a paragon of full disclosure because there is nothing to hide and everything works well when the company identities are inclusive in all emails to recipients.

Accordingly, when the recipients want to make future contact with the company, they need to rest assured that the email correspondence contained the address and 24 hours telephone numbers. Consumers love to do business with the entrepreneurs that are appropriately fully in compliance with the Acceptable Use Policy of the ISP or Mail service providers. Essential example of a responsible email targeting includes a local restaurateur who accumulated 400 email addresses of downtown workers by offering a drawing for a free lunch now sends weekly publication of the lunch specials to these addresses.

One renowned type of email marketing includes direct email marketing that is identical to post office type of email but the only difference being the fastness of direct email marketing. In addition, other kinds of email marketing are transactions via promotional content articles that are contained in the email bulletin. In an email marketing endeavors, other business owner supports piggyback email marketing of which the mode of operation is renting inexpensive column in the email newsletter to convey products or services advertisement.

The procurement department of the online entrepreneurs would normally use money to procure e-mail addresses from other organizations to safely keep in their coffer or databases. Thereafter, in order to generate vast customers, repeatedly the organization would shoot advertisement to all the enlisted e-mail addresses. This system of marketing is infamous as bulk e-mail marketing.

The employees of the online entrepreneurs are infamous for obtaining spontaneous permission from the online user before sending e-mails. One would note that all spontaneous permissions are inclusive in the e-mail messages. This narration depicts opt-in e-mail marketing, known as conveying e-mails to the list of organizational accumulated list of e-mail addresses. The online entrepreneurs are recipient of e-mail newsletters; in addition, they do have the responsibility to peruse online e-mail newsletters in order to assimilate customers' preferences. Society is now aware that e-mail newsletter marketing allows online entrepreneurs to advertise within an e-mail newsletter that reaches their target audience.

The mailing list and Internet profitability confers dominion, power and authority on entrepreneurs. The consequences of misuse of mailing list have the potential to liquidate an online organization. Thus, it behooves the entrepreneur to be extra cautious when using mailing list transmission between company, prospect and customers. Mailing list are normally use by business owners to distribute promotion, newsletter and discussion groups, therefore, any review should indicate that the company is in compliance with the mailing list policy and procedure.

The three common places where mailing lists are conveyed include- promos, newsletter, and discussion group. The policies and procedures that company employ in manipulating promos are the following: (1) determine the purpose of the promo and set concrete goals for results. (2) Establish a system for monitoring results. (3) Formulate a distribution plan for your promotional message. (4) Devise a plan for managing mailing list(s). (5) Generate messages to be delivered (as needed). (6) Deliver messages (as per plan)

(7) Handle response as per plan. (8) Post results planning tool and evaluate performance per plan.

The benchmark that company employ in operating a newsletter are the ensuing: (1) determine the purpose of the newsletter and set concrete goals for results. (2) Establish a system for monitoring results. (3) Formulate a plan for acquiring addresses to add to your distribution list. (4) Develop a plan for managing mailing list(s). (5) Generate messages to (be delivered as needed). (6) Provide messages (periodically as per plan). (7) Handle response as per plan (as needed throughout the day). (8) Post results planning tool and evaluate performance (daily).

The policies and procedures that company utilizes in manipulating a discussion list are the subsequent: (1) describe the purpose of the discussion list and write an introductory message to be sent to new subscribers. (2) Select an appropriate mailing list system and determine the methods you will use in that system to perform the following routine tasks. (3) Import lists of subscribers (to be added). (4) Add individual new subscriber. (5) Eradicate individual subscribers. (6) Remover lists of subscribers. (7) Moderate messages from members. (8) Produce a daily digest of posted messages that can be sent as an option in place of sending individual messages separately. (9) Send messages to the list. (10) Archive posted messages.

We want to develop an email marketing budget in order to help take some of the toil out of the planning and tracking processes. It is advisable to use the Excel worksheet to compute the total contribution margin for each campaign. In case you are not acquainted with that term, here is a brief explanation: Your overall business profits are computed as the difference between total revenues and total expenses. Now, total expenses are made up either of direct costs or fixed costs (also called overhead). Direct costs are expenses you would not acquire if you did not make a sale, such as the cost of the item sold and the cost of shipping. Fixed costs are elements such as rent and utilities that go on whether you sell anything or not. To evaluate the desirability of any particular sale, we need to contemplate only the revenue we get from that sale and the direct costs related to that sale. We can ignore overhead, with one caveat that I will discourse in a minute.

The reason we can disregard overhead is that as long as each sale produces more revenue than its related direct costs, the amount that is left over after paying direct costs either will serve to reduce our overhead bills or (if overhead has already been paid by other sales) will apply to profit. In other words, the revenue we accumulate in excess of direct costs for the item sold is contribution margin, that is, it contributes either to paying fixed costs or to increasing profits.

Once we have sufficient sales from all our business endeavors in total to produce the contribution margin needed to pay all our fixed costs, we can contemplate a new campaign successful if it produces a positive contribution margin, because in this case the contribution goes to profit. If we do not have sufficient sales from all our business activities to pay our overhead, we probably ought to query our entire business plan. Nobody wants to perform all the work of running a business just to lose money.

The entrepreneurs should develop an authentic Web marketing plan, budget, and bring about the implementation. He or she has to coordinate efforts with Internet service providers. In addition, entrepreneurs should conduct a performance evaluation of that plan/budget and adopt continuous improvement program for corrective measures. Meanwhile, in developing a Web marketing plan, the entrepreneurs should embark on planning and tracking the activity on their Web site, and utilize a tool that is quite different from that used to track email.

The primary difference is that you may have several separate strategies at work attracting traffic to the web site. Some of the strategies might even be email-based. Since you may have any number of different strategies in play at any time, there is a real danger that you may discover yourself paying for strategies that manifest results that are not worth their cost. Even if you pay nothing for the strategies in the form of expenses, your time, if wasted, can be even more of a loss. Spending your valuable time on unproductive activities when your intent is to be productive can seriously drain your energies, leaving you with too little energy to carry out the undertakings that do make you money. Planning is a pain in the neck, but Web site developer can really help. When you recognize the purpose of the strategies, think about what you want consumers to do.

Web site developer lets you track sales, subscribers, and three other actions that are left to you to define. I have suggested tracking guestbook sign-ups and requests for additional information. You could also track document downloads, visits to the order page, postings to an online forum or chat room, or any number of other actions. The main point I want to repeat here is that you need to have precise actions in mind as you are designing your Web site. Once you have the Web site in place, you should design specific methods to encourage the actions you want and finally track the actions of your consumers. Using the actual data you collect to assist you make adjustments and select among alternative strategies will, in turn, assist you continuously improve your business system.

Web site developer helps you first as a planning tool, then as a data collection and analysis tool. If you use it as part of your routine, your results cannot help but get better over time.

Correspondingly, a company that intends to embark on an online business should quantify the cost, preplan, set objectives and conduct a feasibility studies. In addition, there is need to quantify sales, average sales, variable cost and document the propose budget in a spreadsheet. This idea is a common knowledge because no company wants to invest in a failing and loss project. The accounting strategy for developing a budget is to quantify the cost of a given project then allocates the fund into the business plan. Even an amateur knows and do conduct a research so that the data derivable will be prorated for the period that ensues.

On the whole, the budget identified should suffice to generate outstanding sales and profit; thus, a company should be fully in compliance with a given budget. On the contrary, web projects are infamous for going over budget

and over the expected timeline. The first thing is to decide
what you are willing to expend on a web site. Then clearly
state what you anticipate in a requirements document.
Bring in several vendors to comment on what they are
capable of doing, and in what timeframe. Always check
background references. It's imperative to negotiate an ongoing rate for services, and not just a rate for the initial web
site. It's not uncommon to want alterations and updates to
the web site. Start on small scale, if the web developer
produces on budget and on time, then you have winner,
otherwise it might be time to cut your losses and move to
another vendor before you start throwing good money after
incompetent web developer.

When the web developers recommends for DHTML effect,
the business owner should deny the request because this
particular software is notorious for permitting Netscape
Navigator to sabotage consumers personal computer. Thus,
the expectation is that the entrepreneurs should continue to
use plain text, prevent the Web developer from utilizing
DHTML effects, and prevent the manifestation of computer
crash. The anticipation of several business communities is
that Web site developer will create the menu-bars so tiny and
insert this menu-bars in the proper locality. Conversely,
business practitioner should discourage a performance of
creativity on menu-bars because this will disgust, discourage
and expel potential consumers from the Web site. In
addition, entrepreneurs should require the Web developer to
incorporate the same menu-bars on all the pages of the Web
site. This is excellent because it will simplify updating file
and contents of the menu-bars. In addition, that menu-bars
on the footer or bottom of all pages should also be in place
because this will aid visitors when scrolling to the end
destination. Besides, I question the lengthy Web page that
has side effect of disappearance. Hence, an entrepreneur
should remedy the situation by replicating the horizontal
menu-bars just above the footer element. In addition,
instead of using icon or arrow for the link, company should
concentrate on a written word because this will simplify Web
site navigation system. In brief, entrepreneurs are reminded

that menu-bars must take consumers to the action page whenever a single click is pressed, because online business are meant to be a forum for the visitors to elicit buying actions.

Similarly, below are some likely actions you may wish to incite: (a) Place an order for products via an e-commerce link. (b) place an order for products via email, (c) place an order for products via fax, (d) ask for more information, (e) sign up for a newsletter subscription, (f) sign up for a drawing or other contest, (g) sign your guest book, (h) call you on the phone, (i) send you a fax requesting information, (j) respond to a survey questionnaire, (k) submit a suggestion for products or services, (l) schedule an appointment, (m) apply for a job with your company, (n) offer to sell you something, (o) request that a sales representative get in touch with them, (p) download a document or other file. By no means are you limited to just these actions. My point is that you must decide what you want potential customers to do before you construct a page. Then and only then can you deliberately cause the outcomes you want. Part of the technique for getting potential customers to do what you want them to do is making it simple for them to act. One key to that goal is to make the action page only a (single click) away from any location in your Web site. However, the menu-bars are indispensable element to Web site navigation system. Accordingly, web developers customarily allocate menu-bars at the pinnacle of the web page otherwise on the left locality of the web page. Equally important, the web developers should create menu-bars with a simple text to make navigation comfortable. As an illustration, the outstanding attributes of menu-bars are the following: (a) tiny menu-bars, (b) word only, (c) never use icons, (d) menu-bars is stationary, (e) first level menu-bars are accessible, (f) replicate menu-bar at the base of the web page, and (g) menu-bars navigate users to their destination. Conclusively, menu-bars should simplify online user intentions speedily and effortlessly.

A site map can be a nice addition to your Web site, especially when your site propagates to include many pages.

Typical site maps let prospective customers perceive a sort of (table of contents) view of your Web site, with each entry a clickable hyperlink. Good site maps assist prospective customers see how each page relates to other pages in the site and, as a result, assist visitors quickly find just what they are searching for. MS FrontPage offers two potent automatic tools for building a site map. For a single Web site, you can use the Front-Page (Table of Contents) component. For larger sites including sub-webs (FP webs within a web) and wide page listings, the (Categories) element will let you automate more complex site maps. The really nice thing about using these Front-Page elements to build your site map is that your map is automatically updated as you revise pages, potentially saving you lots of manual tweaking. Conversely, a sitemap is a web page that performs as a table of contents for your web site. The more your website expands, the more complex it may be for users to find information. A nice search interface can assist prospective customers find what they are looking for, but a sitemap permit a prospective customer know all the areas of your web site. Your web site may contain some obscure gems that the prospective customers did not know about, and a sitemap is a great place for the user to discover these types of web pages.

There is a notation that Web site blog place is actually a forum for the discussions of anomalies and concerns as well as the virtual environment in which visitors and companies rapport in unison. In communicating forums, the business owners have marvelous opportunity to inspire visitors to relay issues of discussion by participant to relation, colleagues, friend, relatives, neighbors and coworkers. Hobby sites make great utilization of the threaded discussion forum, and you may also discover it valuable for providing help to your prospective customers. If your prospective customers are interested enough to participate in an online discussion, they can actually provide you with assistance by answering the questions others may have-and, in the bargain, you may learn how people really feel about your business. If you do decide to put up a discussion forum, I suggest that you promote it to your prospective customers and that you observe it consistently.

An online business may have contract with ASP services for package trailing, group support, searching support, shopping cart services, engagement scheduling, or online bill payment services. The merit of connections to other services like ASP is on the minds of several online small business owners. Thus, cost conscious online small business owners might as well take the benefits that are accessible from online free services. Similarly, there are numerous benefit when you have ASP as your vendor, further, the following are the provisions: (a) instruction are given for embedding HTML tags to construct link and form on Web site (b) ASP provides HTML code snippets (c) ASP provides great customers service (d) ASP provides email support. Though, some forms are merely hand-off points to third-party providers, such as shopping cart systems or discussion forum providers. It's much more economical to use a third party service than to embed thing such as a shopping cart from scratch. Even if you did embed an e-commerce site, you'd still require to communicate with a third party to process your payment. This would generally involve a form posting to the other service's web site.

I encourage entrepreneurs to take advantages of the free graphics provided by several web sites for the purposes of maximum site enhancement. However, he advised business owners to peruse the term of service also cautioned about violating the letter of the law. An entrepreneur should be compliant with the copyright law in order to avoid costly liability. Thus, before a graphic user take ownership of the free graphic he or she should obtain clearance from the web site owner. Similarly, the administrators are encouraged not to revisit online to download the same graphic image contents but to reuse or resize the graphic image. Online users dislike slow web site, however, frequent download of graphic image causes slow loading of online pages. Accordingly, I acknowledge that some companies that frequently download graphic image discourages return visit of consumers to the web site. In short, the explicit strategies to manage graphic for maximum enhancement is to apply width or length specifications.

To maximize profitability the online entrepreneurs are required to embed current news reports, sports, weather, jokes, comedy, stock quotes and other interesting media clip that enhances the Web site because this have potential to promote consumers revisit or repurchase from the Web site. However, Stickiness is all about incessant revisit of visitors to a particular Web site. An example of sticky Web site is the one that contains thought provoking discussion. As we all know, people prefer forums for the discussion of issues and concerns as well as the virtual environment in which any such issues are raised thus people will always come to update dialogue and cross check correspondence. Consequently, the following are the signal that a Web site promote stickiness: (a) web site that contains persistent upload, (b) interesting contents, (c) presentation that drive revisit of visitors, and (d) stock or News sites where people revisits to obtain daily information.

What is the definition of streaming? Streaming is a modern technology that individual employ to playback audio and video files from the famous online web page. Streaming is popularly known as web casting that support live or pre-recorded program. To illustrate, the following are the advantages of using streaming audio and video: (a) you only need tiny bandwidth, (b) you only need computer with 56k modem, (c) allow small computer buffer system, (d) allow cursory playback of video and audio files, and (e) deliver compelling messages to potential customers on the web site. In addition, streaming audio and video: (a) provides cheap video advertisement, (b) provides cheap audio advertisement, (c) allow global education, and (d) provides audio/video clips for people to watch directly from the Web site. Moreover, (a) a user can view PowerPoint slides from the web server, (b) a user can view the slideshow from the web server, and (c) a user can view software tutorial program from the server. Similarly, when the Internet Service Providers perform the corrective actions, for instance, on band width limitation then they are able to offers streaming audio and video to the Web consumers. Streaming audio and video enables you to broadcast video clips via the browser window. On the whole, the following examples are representatives of what this streaming technology offers: enable web content; live chat room, video feed and online radio.

In developing online content, primarily, the language used by an organization should be easy to understand, attractive and enables consumer retention. Meanwhile, an absolute care is encouraged to ensure that company does not ignore the complication, cost and implications of online content delivery systems. Thus, an entrepreneur should enlist the services of cost efficient Web developer. Entrepreneurs should take steps to communicate effectively to the Web site developers to construct the content for ease of updating correction and maintenance. Meanwhile, entrepreneur should institute appropriate provision for developing content that should be disseminated to consumers through a variety of available media: for example, new letters, posters, emails, questionnaires, presentation, audio and video clips. In brief, some authority have expressed that business owners are encouraged to actively delegate monitoring functions to certain employee of the company because this will elicit locus of control in the aspect of developing and maintaining the site content.

If you have strategies that comprise selling products online and you expect to offer more than a few dozen products and/or product variations, I recommend that you do it right: build a database as the foundation for your Web site. Although, as in the case of content-rich sites, a database Web site can be very obscured and costly, you can attain a great deal of power and productive benefit from a relatively simple database Web site, and for very little money. At the most basic level, you should be able to get an MS Access database comprising of product records with quantity, price, description, product ID, product picture, and several other product-specific variables set up as a stand-alone database for less than $500. Linking up this database as a back-end to a dynamic catalog Web site should less expensive than an additional $1,000. This is not a shopping cart, I am just communicating about a means for presenting all the items. If you desire to offer shopping cart functionality, contact the e-commerce ASPs and ask them how you can best supply your backend so that it will integrate seamlessly with their shopping cart and online payment systems. By using an e-commerce provider, you may be able to save the $1,000 additional development costs and just use the standard services provided by the ASP.

Furthermore, a database Web site lets you deliver content that is always current, without your constantly having to edit the pages in your Web site. Updating a Web site that is equipped with a database back-end is as simple as updating the database. In a perpetual inventory system, you have to update your database anyway to keep track of your inventory items, and in a properly constructed database Web site, your inventory database becomes the source of all the product information presented on the Web site. When visitors search for a product or call up a category listing, all the information they see is extracted from the database and presented on the fly. That means every time you update your inventory database, your Web site is updated as well. The simplest such database Web site uses a separate database that is maintained on the local PC just for the purpose of supporting the Web site. This database is updated as needed and then uploaded to the host computer (using FTP Dr FrontPage) where it overwrites the old database copy. Such a separate Web site database does require separate maintenance, in addition to' the work you already do in supporting your primary inventory database. But if your existing inventory database is highly integrated into your management information system, a separate database might offer the only cost-effective solution. Revising a large and sophisticated database system can cost lots of money.

Organizations are encouraged to employs this type of passive method to induce prospect to find your website. The two common methods for producing Web site traffic exist, for instance, the passive and active strategies by which you can help prospects to locate or drive prospective to the Web site during their active search activities. In a traditional business plan you might help prospects discover you by first selecting a name for your business that communicates clearly what you offer, and then by choosing an appropriate location, advertising in the yellow pages. In addition, putting up a sign on the street, establishing a referral network of complementary businesses and paying to be listed in relevant directories and guidebooks. Meanwhile, there are several ways to provide solicitation on the Web site in order to encourage online prospects to participate in the purchase of the products or services. To illustrate, the following attributes does signifies how to help prospects locate a particular company: (a) own domain name, (b) enlisted on appropriate host service, (c) administer search engine positioning, (d) oversee pay-per-click listings, (e) managing search engine, (f) use directory listing descriptions, (g) own reciprocal link arrangements with complementary businesses, (h) join exceptional interest directories.

Equally important, as marketing component, your domain name should be selected based on three criteria: brand identity, keyword presence, and recall-ability. In the quest of assisting prospective consumers find you, the focus should be (capitalize on your brand identity), if you possess a brand name that has value, ascertain that the brand name appears in the domain name. For example, IBM. com and Microsoft.com. If your brand is not widely known among prospective customers and not likely to become so, select a domain name based on one or both of the other criteria. How do you know if your brand name has value in an online context? If your prospective customers are likely to search for the products or services you offer by entering your brand name in a search box, then your brand has value. In addition, keyword presence should be the focal point, thus, if you have weak brand identity, then ascertain the domain name you select contains one or, better yet, several highly relevant keywords. Keywords are the words inserted by Web users when they want to discover something on the Web. Similarly, if you do not have a brand name to use and you do not have keywords to use in your domain name, I suggest that you implement an easy to remember domain name, if you do integrate keywords; you can procure a memorable domain name. Only the small business owner may decide to select domain name that identifies with keyword presence, brand identity and recall-ability. In addition, business owners may exercise his or her discretion to campaign with a well-known brand identity. For instance, we have the legendary IBM. com and Microsoft.com. On the whole, keyword presence should be the focal point when a company lacks brand identity.

The banner ads, those narrow ads that appear across the Web page usually near the top, remain the main advertising system used on the Web today. Big companies and small companies alike routinely use banner ads to promote visits to their Web sites. There are two rudimentary kinds of banner ad systems: free systems and pay systems. In a free system, the banner ad system operator implement an advertisement server program that controls what advertisement gets presented on the web sites. Hundreds and even thousands of Web-site developers place links to the advertisement server on their Web sites. Each time a visitor accesses a linked page, the advertisement server delivers a banner advertisement to be displayed in the space provide on the Web page. Free systems operate on the principle of reciprocity. The largest such free system is the Link-Exchange Banner Network that claims to have 400,000 sites in their system. In the Link-Exchange system, members must depict two advertisement for each advertisement of their own that gets depicted once, so the operator is selling half of the ad inventory. Not a bad deal-for the web developers. (Microsoft owns Link-Exchange.).

To demonstrate, the following are the few examples of the systems that may drive prospects to the Web site: (a) free systems, (b) pay systems and (c) servers programs. The small business owners are encouraged to actively participate in the free Link-Exchange banner network because there is no cost to the company and this will maximize the financial viability of the company. The basic solicitation mediums that drive prospective consumers to the Web site are the display of banner advertisement, pop-ups, newsletters and promos. Meanwhile, one thing is worthy of representation; prospects solicitation officially endorsed by the entrepreneurs or companies (such as banners advertisement), release of this advertisement are without the assent of online users. However, in conventional advertising, once you ascend onto the Web and begin using email in your business, you will probably continue to use your existing promotional tools, such as newspaper advertising, flyers, business cards, and the like. Don't stop unless the cost of the techniques are exorbitant. Add your Internet access information to these conventional promotional media and messages. Put your Web address, twitter address, and email address on every message: (a) in every advertisement both on- and offline, (b) on every employee's business card, (c) on the side of your delivery trucks, (d) on your custom imprinted check-out bags. In addition, (a) on custom imprinted advertising specialty give-a-ways, (b) on signs throughout the store, (c) on employee uniforms, (d) on your store sign, (e) on billboard ads, on the side of your building, and (f) on the front door. Ascertain that your customers know how to reach you by every means you offer: phone, fax, email, Web, twitter, street address, postal address. Think warm. Help your prospective consumers find you using whatever method they prefer.

The secret to getting maximum advantage from all your Internet-enabled marketing efforts is to work toward a fully integrated business system. As you consider each Internet strategy, determine how that strategy will merge into your current business plan. Adding email promos can assist to generate inquiries that you can then follow up just as you do your current inquiries that arrive by mail or telephone. Distributing a newsletter online via email that links to a full color brochure site with relevant articles and other current content can replace part or all of your current newsletter disseminated via regular mail. The addition of color and more widespread materials can improve the outcome from the newsletter, whether it is designed to produce name recognition, sales leads, or sales orders. While roughly half of all businesses currently have Web sites, few actually sell anything online. But selling is just a part of the business plan, which includes commenting your story, providing communications channels between you and your customers, educating customers, delivering products, dealing with post-purchase communications, finding resources you need in your business, locating employees, locating customers and prospects, following up on leads and setting appointments, entertaining customers and prospects, handling your operations, and on and on-there is a lot to do. Carefully select from the myriad tools accessible on the Internet those that promise to assist you better solve your predicament and better serve your customers. You have now seen a foretaste of the online world and all the magnificent things that become promising because it exists. Think of the Internet as a box of tools, each with particular capabilities. Your toolbox may be filled with promising potentials now, but the options will only expand as we move forward in time. Integrate each new tool into your system. If it will not fit, discard it and try another until you find the solution you seek. By incorporate these wonderful new capabilities into your existing, traditional business system, the possibilities for your business are excellent definitely. Consequently, to accrue financial feasibility in the Internet marketing program, business practitioner should vigorously integrate product, reliability, durability, services delivery, accessibility, and Web site appearance and employee knowledge. Time is of the essence for companies to effectively promote global selling and trading. Companies should develops and convey marketing presentation via all technological media to the online consumers and cohorts. There following strategies will bring about maximum benefits: (a) contributes to online marketing effectiveness, (b) resolves both short time and long-term marketing issues, (c) develops and maintains relations with consumers by propounding client relations program, and (d) blend or integrate technology tool into the marketing structure.

The owners of personal service businesses should ensure that the entire customers' relationship are coordinated and administered in an efficient, courtesy or professional manner to elicit customer satisfaction. In the meantime, personal service customers accept behavior patterns illustrated by repeat purchases that are very analogous and that occur on a reliable schedule. Once your personal service business has procured a customer base, you can be guaranteed that your customers will be back again and again, purchasing the same things you offer in the same quantities-that is, unless you dissatisfy them by changing your offerings in a way the customers do not like. Typically, because personal service customers are so loyal and change to a new personal service business only rarely, it can take years to build such a business. Moreover, such customer loyalty is fragile, and you can extinguish such a business in a matter of weeks if you fail to maintain constancy in all your dealings with customers. Once you have a customer base, in a personal service business the customers are yours to lose. They will stay as long as you treat them with decorum and their lives do not require that they leave. However, the main operational challenge in a personal service business is maintaining stability. Make sure the only surprises your prospective consumers have are happy little treats. Be cautious about big changes-even changes (for the better) can cost you. As you reflect how to utilize the Internet in your personal service business, be careful not to remove components of your business that are imperative to customers. Instead, offer Internet improvements that make your service better by providing alternatives along with traditional components. When and if your customers move to the alternative strategy, you may consider discontinuing the old strategy. Just be cautious not to push your customers too hard in the new direction. Personal service businesses have to work really rigid to get new customers. For these businesses, customer loyalty cuts both ways. People who are not your customers are the customers of your competitors, and most of the customers of your competitors are complex to dislocate. Your competitors will commit mistakes, though, and when they do, you must be there to gain their estranged customers before somebody else does. That means you need a high profile in the community from which your prospective customers come. For this purpose, a constant, low-level advertising program is usually best. A big sign on a busy street, a small ad in the newspaper every day, signs on bus stop benches, a regular coupon inserted in the weekly shopper, all can assist you to keep your name in front of your prospective consumers so that when they get ticked off at your competitor, they naturally contemplate of you.

When people make big-decision purchases (cars, appliances, homes, motorcycles and the like) loyalty becomes mostly irrelevant. The big-decision purchases are made infrequently, and so the rapport between your business and the customer is quite objective. That means you must create an operation that instantly converts prospects into buyers while they are in your store. If your business system lets prospective consumer get away, they are gone for good nearly every time. In the sales business the adage says, (callbacks don't make greenbacks).Your business might offer the inexpensive price, the best selection, free delivery, and more, yet still suffer from the attrition of the customers, if your operation is not implemented specifically to close the sale on the first visit. I am not advocating that your sales people pressurize customers or resort to abusive sales practices. If you do that, your business will suffer from lots of bad-mouthing, both by customers who bought and those who did not purchase, because they all felt they were treated badly. Too much bad word-of-mouth publicity and your business will become a local pariah that most prospects will shun.

The problem is that prospective consumers who visit you once assume they have no more to learn from you, and so, as they continue through the buying process, they never come back. This means you only focus on who are just about ready to purchase when they first walk into your store. Those prospects who are just getting started in their decision process are almost certainly lost when they leave. (a) By utilizing the Internet to keep in touch, you can remain right by their sides as your prospective customers worry over their big purchase decision. Using private email rapports, twitter and newsletters to keep your name before them, you can become a cordial personal assistant as they work through the process in their own good time. Email and the Web let you begin and end each day by renewing and managing all your open contacts in a way you never could before. Since you are a proficient in your industry and in your products, you can offer tips and new knowledge for their consideration. You can elicit their thoughts and apprehensions as they muddle their way through their decisions. (b) By keeping in touch and becoming a trusted advisor who engages in helping prospective consumers reach a satisfactory conclusion, the chances are greatly maximized that you will get the sale and some great word-of-mouth publicity after the sale as well. Using email, twitter, and the Web will almost definitely put you well ahead of your competitors today. These practices will become routine in the next few years, so your only practical choice is either to lead or to get dragged along. (c) Besides keeping your prospective consumers in the loop, your Web site can also assist you to get more customers into your store and help you educate some of them before they arrive so they are closer to being ready to purchase when they get there. Once prospective consumers are in the store, you can even utilize the Web to walk them through competitors' online sites, to assist them comparison shop, demonstrating that you really are offering the best deal. For this to work of course, you really must offer the best deal. By setting up an online credit application-or allowing a retail credit organization to do so via an ASP link in your Web site-you can offer your prospective consumers instant credit approval. You can utilize an online scheduling ASP to schedule deliveries so that, before customer sign, customers can know precisely when they will get the goods. (d) Using Internet tools can enable you to create a complete marketing system that, together with your traditional tools, will produce a closing percentage sure to defeat your strongest competitors.

A debate currently endures to rage over whether or not online shopping will supersede offline shopping. I believe that online shopping will eventually displace catalog shopping and some small part of traditional shopping as well, but your shopping -destination business will become sturdy than ever if you climb aboard the Internet express. Shopping-destination consumers repeatedly visit lots of stores without buying anything. Next to observing television, shopping is the most popular form of amusement in America-and, 1 suspect, in most developed countries in the world. Shopping is fun! We love to look at, feel, and visualize ourselves using or wearing the wonderful shopping goods we find in malls, downtowns, and other places where we find shopping-destination vendors. Let me also augment that men like shopping too-no, not for frilly and trivial stuff like clothes-but for real man stuff, like guns and tools and trucks and hardware

Likewise, once you have potential customers email addresses, send consistent announcements (once a week to once a month) inviting customers to visit your Web site. Once they are there, show them the brand new designs you have in stock, show them all the colors, and tell them the prices, the sizes, the materials from which the clothes are made. Inform them the names of the sheep from which the wool was shorn and present the autobiography and pictures of the designers and the chateaus in the French Alps in which they live. Show your potential customers the appropriate accessories; assist them see themselves dressed in the new items. On your Web site, you are not limited to a mannequin. Why not show a hundred mannequins, all fully accessorized to show the various ways the items in your store can work for your potential customers to improve their social lives, get promotions, and win fame, love, and fortune? Your suppliers or vendors already have done most of the work. Ask if they have the images you want for your site, in electronic form. If they do, embed them to your site; then inform your newsletter recipients about your exciting brand new offerings and give them a link to get them there. Using the Internet in this way, you can greatly maximize the reach of your online store by embedding an online storefront-a catalog Web site-that lets you present brand new items to potential customers who might otherwise never revisit your store to see them. Use the Web site to drive potential customers into your store.

ABOUT THE AUTHOR

Dr. Ebenezer A. Robinson is an author, professor, mentor, motivational speaker, coach, writer, consultant, researcher, advocate for higher education, and is a California State University Alumnus. He holds an MBA and PhD degree in Business Administration and Electronic Commerce. His call is to educate, motivate, teach, train and empower others for life success. Dr. Robinson has over 30 years of corporate America, government, industry, entrepreneurship, education, consulting, executive director, management accounting, and training experience.

References:

Akinola, A. (2006). Targeting your email.
http://www.seochat.com/c/a/Website-Marketing-
Help/Targeting-Your-Email/

Ab Hamid, N. R. (2005). E-CRM: Are we there yet? Journal
of American academy of Business Cambridge. Hollywood:
Vol.6, Iss. 1; pg. 51, 7 pgs
http://proquest.umi.com.proxy1.ncu.edu/pqdweb/?index.

Bergman, T., P. (2002). The essential guide to web strategy
for entrepreneurs. Prentice Hall. Upper Saddle River, New
Jersey.

Bergman, T., P. (2002). The essential guide to web strategy
for entrepreneurs. Prentice Hall. ISBN 0-13-062111-0.

Caffery, L., Crew-Wegner, K., Reid, W., & Wootton, R.
(2004). Automatic message handling for a national
counseling service. Journal of Telemedicine and
Telecare. London: Vol.10 pg. 18, 4 pgs. Retrieved from
http://proquest.umi.com.proxy1.ncu.edu/pqdweb/?index.

Cho, C., H., and Khang, H., (2006). The state of
internet-related research in communications, marketing,
and advertising: Journal of advertising. Provo:
Vol.35, Iss. 3; pg. 143, 21 pgs.
http://proquest.umi.com.proxy1.ncu.edu/pqdweb/?inde

Gebhardt, J (2009). Intellectual property on the Internet.
http://wrt.syr.edu/uc/archivedsyllabi
/other/skordili/classes/305/gebhard2.htm

Gates, B. (1999). Business at the speed of thought. Warner
Books.

Korper, Steffano, Ellis, Juanita (2001). The e-commerce
book, building the e-empire Academic Press. ISBN:
0124211615

Laudon, K. C. and Traver, C. G. (2006). E-commerce,
business, technology, and society (3rd Ed.). Prentice Hall.
Upper Saddle River, New Jersey.

Millman, G. J. (2004). Keeping data under lock
& key. Financial executive, Vol. 20 Issue 5, p20-22, 3p,
http://web.ebscohost.com.proxy1.ncu.edu/ehost/pdf?vid

Moshkovich, H., Mechitov, A., and Olson, D., (2005). Infusion of electronic commerce into the information systems curriculum. The journal of computer information systems. Stillwater

Pride, William, and Ferrell, O.C. (2003) Marketing concepts and strategies. Prentice Hall.

Rayport, Jefferey, Jaworkski, Bernard, J. (2005). E-Commerce. New York, NY: McGraw-Hill Higher Education. ISBN 0-07246521-2.

Turban, E., Lee, J., King, D., Chung, H. M. (2004).Electronic commerce, A managerial perspective. Prentice-Hall.

Dr. Ebenezer A. Robinson, PhD